"Deeg-In"

with Family and Friends

Turtle Brownie Cake, page 189

Best of the Best presents

"Deeg-In"

with Family and Friends

MarkCharles Misilli

QUAIL RIDGE PRESS

Preserving America's Food Heritage

ISBN 978-1-934193-91-4
First Edition
Printed in the USA

Book Development by:
The Culinary Palette, Ronda DiGuglielmo
Land & Associates, Donna Land

Food Photography by Alison Miksch

Design by Jack Murray Design

Published by Quail Ridge Press
and Great Chefs International

www.quailridge.com
www.greatchefsinternational.com

Dedication

Each of us has a unique upbringing that's shaped by many factors. And food is one of the most important. No matter where you grew up or how old you are, I bet some of your happiest memories of childhood have food in them.

Childhood has to end, but the foods we grew up on, the ones that marked holidays, filled the house with wonderful smells, and that made dinner something to look forward to, can stay with us for a lifetime.

This book is filled with recipes that created memories and brought joy to my friends' and family's childhoods.

For myself, an unforgettable part of growing up was hearing my grandma Muzia say, when we sat down ready to eat our meal, **"DEEG-IN!"** For those of you who weren't lucky enough to know her, that's "Dig in!" in a thick French accent.

This book is dedicated to my beloved Grandmere, aka Meme Muzia, my mom's mom. She will forever live in my heart, my traditions and my cooking. May the recipes shared here become part of your family traditions and the fabric which makes up your life.

All my best, happy cooking and **"DEEG-IN!"**

MCM

Grandmere's Broccoli and
Cauliflower Gratin, page 170

Contents

Rita's Christmas Eve Onion Soup—
a French Tradition, page 146

Foreword

by Gwen McKee

MarkCharles Misilli and I have been friends for a long time, mainly from so often bumping into each other (I mean that literally in the busy QVC studio) for years on cook shows, travel shows, and the occasional after-hours escape times, when we have some laughs with mutual friends. I love being around someone so sharp and clever and fun. MarkCharles is very much connected to the food world in so many ways, including a kazillion handy products that make getting around in the kitchen so much easier...and I can vouch for a whole slew of them, that's for sure.

Besides being "The Kitchen Gadget Guru," as some refer to him, MarkCharles is a fantastic designer, stylist, and cook. He has excellent taste, too. I love when he comes to my cookbook table after a show for a nibble of something that he "couldn't resist." I am amazed at his ability to size something up, and to be able to tell you how to make the most of it, whether it's a selling point, or a sauce or glaze tip, or simply that a particular wine would go so well with this particular dish.

Gwen McKee and MarkCharles behind the scenes at QVC

Years ago, when I was working on the *QVC Family Cookbook*, MarkCharles was not only quick to respond to my request for a recipe, but he was excited about it. And a superb recipe it was! And when I included a picture of him I took at the studio, he was absolutely thrilled. He was thereafter an ambassador of that cookbook, something I was grateful for then, and still am.

MarkCharles has learned a lot about cooking from his French mother and Italian father, and an extended family who love to cook and eat. Now it is time to share some of these family recipes, and to introduce his fans to just how good he is at creating delectable dishes. In this cookbook that literally goes the gamut from simple surprises to gourmet presentations, the thing I like about *"Deeg-In"* the most is that it encourages you to push your kitchen creativity to experience new and delicious flavors to give your daily cooking a new dimension. I knew it would be exceptional, but I am awed—though not surprised—at how interesting and inviting these recipes are.

MarkCharles' recipes go beyond good. Not only does he give you careful step-by-step instructions with a shopping list of ingredients, but he also provides you with tips on how to present these dishes to make any dining experience more memorable.

Quail Ridge Press is proud to publish and put our "Best of the Best" seal of approval on *"Deeg-In" with Family and Friends*. Way to go, MarkCharles!

Gwen McKee

Gwen McKee is a cookbook publisher, author, editor, and frequent QVC guest. Her company, Quail Ridge Press, has published over 200 cookbooks.

Introduction

Seeing, eating and connecting

I've always liked shrimp cocktail served in a martini glass. There's something elegant about it, something inviting, something that says there's more to this dish than cooked shellfish and a squirt of sauce. Maybe there's even a hint that there's more to this existence than the everyday and the ordinary. Shrimp cocktail in a martini glass is like a window into a happier life.

Am I making too much of this? I don't think so.

Food can be part of a least-common-denominator existence, prepared without joy and consumed without pleasure, without much thought of any kind, really. And if you take the time to look, you'll see it happening just that way, all around us, every day.

Or food can be wonderful, truly nourishing to the spirit as well as the body. It can contribute to the special chemistry that binds together friends, lovers, families. It can be the catalyst that changes us from strangers to people who feel a warm connection. Food can bring human beings together in deep and lasting ways.

I love to cook, to share both the making of meals and the enjoyment of the result. So part of the idea behind this book is to share with you a collection of superb recipes, each one kitchen tested and proven to produce a pleasing dish. If you love this food too, I'll have succeeded.

But there's more to this.

Well-prepared and well-presented food is a treat for all five senses. (You might think hearing doesn't apply, but it does. Who can listen to the mellow bubbling of a casserole hot from the oven without feeling real anticipation?) Besides letting you in on these great recipes, I also hope to encourage you to think about presenting what you prepare in ways that please all the senses. Why not make something as enjoyable as eating a complete experience?

Grandmere

11

More about this later.

One thing you won't find here is a recipe for shrimp cocktail. I'd rather let that stand as an invitation to your own creativity in cooking and meal presentation. Here's hoping that you'll find a way to offer your favorites in ways that speak to you just as powerfully as that one does to me.

The European way, the American way

My family history is a little out of the ordinary for a 21st-century American, and the way I relate to food grows directly out of that. I'm heir to an immigrant experience more like what many people experienced a hundred years ago.

Grandpere and Grandmere Wiertelosz

In my case, the reverberations of French and Italian culture are close enough to remain very resonant. Two generations ago my family was still in Europe. And when they came to the United States, they cooked, drank and ate in characteristically European ways.

The way they worked in the kitchen was worlds away from America's culture of convenient food. In our house, sauces would simmer richly on the stove all day. The selection of foods was typically European, too. Other kids on the block might be tucking in to macaroni and cheese. At our house, we'd be sitting down to rabbit, escargot, and fancy veal dishes.

Grandpa and Grandma Misilli

This all peaked on Sundays, when the whole day would be devoted to preparing a special dinner. Every member of the family was expected to take part in getting this feast together, and we all did. It's a wonderful memory—the house full of those wonderful smells, the anticipation of the terrific meal to come. And the payoff would come when it was all ready and my grandmother would call out "DEEG-IN!" To those of you not up on your Mediterranean-accented English, that's "Dig in!" That's when all of us sat down to eat together.

I've embraced those traditions, but I've also sought ways to adapt and evolve them, making them more my own. Whatever heritage we claim, it can't provide every answer for contemporary living—how could it, after all? The secret is to find what has merit and meaning, and bring that into our lives today. That's as true in the kitchen as it is in every aspect of living.

Grandma Misilli (Nonna)

In my own children, I see some of the conflicts that I lived through while growing up with a life in multiple cultures. Tradition can be a burden for the young, making them feel grounded in a way they don't especially like. My children naturally have a different view of the world than I have. And after all, they're entitled to a rebellion of their own. I'm not worried. They'll come around.

Souvenirs of the table

One thing we're feeding when we eat is memory. Here's an example. When I was a boy, my French mother's Christmas Eve specialty was onion soup. It was excellent, distinguished from lesser examples by subtle inclusions of oregano and white wine—not to mention love. (You'll find it on page 146.)

Onion soup for Christmas? To an American kid of a certain age, that time of life when belonging is especially important, this seemed needlessly alien, maybe even weird—certainly not in keeping with this country's traditional holiday meals. But my mother was French through and through, born in Cannes and raised in Paris. She had a different view of things. "We have our own traditions," she said.

If there's a better way to connect with tradition and make memories than by enjoying delicious food, I don't know what it is. Memory tells me that, whatever else I know about Christmas Eve, it tastes like good onion soup.

Now presenting

As marvelous as the European way of cooking is, I'm afraid there's at least one serious hole in it. In my family, at least, there was always a tendency to neglect the presentation of the superb things that came out of the pot.

I'll admit that the old people had a point. First and last, cooking must be about the food. I don't agree, though, that presentation doesn't matter. My spin is that everything matters. Great flavor, yes. Tantalizing textures, of course. Magnificent aroma—well, that goes without saying. Even what we hear is to the point. Not for nothing do advertising executives talk about selling the sizzle, not the steak.

Dad and Nonno in Italy sharing a glass of wine

Without ignoring basic matters of flavor and quality, I think how food looks is something you just can't neglect if you want to succeed as a cook. Love comes in at the eye, Yeats said, and I think it's just as true of our excitement over our dinners.

This is no great revelation, maybe, but you'd be surprised how many people don't get it. In particular, they don't seem to register that what restaurants do to produce a great experience for their customers works just as well at home.

When you're throwing a dinner party, present to impress. Always. Unpack your best linens and fold the napkins in a striking way. Serve the different courses in unexpected vessels. Play up the colors in the food and the wine. Dine by candlelight. Look for creative ways to address every aspect of the dining experience, just as restaurateurs do. Make it great at every level, and people will be thrilled to be invited the next time.

About the recipes and their organization

Let's take some time now to discuss the way this cookbook is organized, and what's behind the recipes you'll find here.

The chapter layout divides the year into its seasons, and presents food and drink appropriate to each part of the year. One of the leading trends that's influenced many cooks in recent years—professionals and amateurs alike—is the drive to

Mom (right) and her parents

purchase local produce. Of course this is a great idea—it often produces better meals, and it can be a "green" way to eat since less energy is expended in bringing the food to you.

But eating locally is also a key to eating seasonally. In developing the recipes, I've tried to think about what's available to Americans season by season. Most of us will have access to fresh garden greens in the springtime, crisp apples close to home in the fall, and so on. Whether you're using one of my recipes or trying something else, you'll find it a little easier to cook with seasonal success if you look for the good things that grow, figuratively or literally, in your backyard.

Cooking seasonally does another wonderful thing for us—it puts us directly in touch with the celebrations that succeed one another all through the year. In this sense, I'm drawn to my European roots again. If you've spent time in Italy, you know that one saint's festival follows close on the heels of another, with more coming soon after, right through the whole calendar.

Any occasion is good enough to justify doing something special at the table—and maybe turning it into an even bigger celebration. When you do that, do it with a healthy measure of imagination and your whole heart.

Not every recipe fits into a quarterly plan. The fifth chapter of this book contains what I call seasonless recipes. These are timeless favorites waiting to please you no matter what time of year you prepare them.

This selection is meant to be for everyone. It presents a very wide range of ingredients, textures, colors and flavors, not to mention national origins of the dishes. You'll discover salads and sandwiches, main courses and side dishes, opulent desserts and quick treats, smoothies and sophisticated cocktails.

Grandpere Eryck

Dad carving our first Thanksgiving turkey

Every one of these recipes is kitchen tested, and all of them produce results that people really like. Still, I want to encourage people to use this cookbook more as a guide than a prescription. You should try your own take on every recipe you prepare. (To help you with this, many entries include tips for variations on the recipe's main theme.)

Moving beyond strict recipe details is part of learning and growing in the kitchen. To make that easier, every recipe includes space for notes. This book won't really be yours until you've scribbled in a bunch of personal opinions and observations.

Some final thoughts

So now it's time to share some concluding observations. You'll notice that the majority of these recipes can be prepped and cooked in less than an hour. I will always honor the patient, exacting elders in my family who taught me old-world, day-long ways of making unforgettable meals. But, like it or not, contemporary Americans seldom can spare five hours to fix dinner.

The trick for me has been to seek dishes and methods that will approximate those slower effects without introducing impossible cook times. I believe I've succeeded in this. We should not hurry at the cutting board or the stove. Cooking can be understood as a ritual, something preparatory to the necessary and joyful sacrament of eating. If you can possibly avoid rushing through the prep phases of these recipes, please do. Take your time. Food preparation, when it's done right, ought to be more than a means to the end of putting food on the table. It should be something worth doing in itself. Even more, take your time when you eat the food you make with help from this book. Having a twenty-minute sit-down meal with your family can be a meditation and a revelation. Attend to the aromas and the flavors of the food. Share the pleasures of conversation, and respond to what your tablemates direct to you. Relax. Savor the moment.

Now that's good eating.   MCM

Pantry List

Listed on the following three pages are the ingredients that are used in the recipes in this cookbook.

Baking Items

apple pie filling

baking mix

baking powder

baking soda

canola oil

chocolate chips

chocolate cookie pie crust

chocolate sprinkles

coconut

confectioners' sugar

cornstarch

dried cherries

dried cranberries

dried mixed fruit

flour

fudge brownie mix

light brown sugar

orange extract

pumpkin quick bread mix

raisins

sugar

unsweetened chocolate

unsweetened cocoa

vanilla cake mix

whipped white frosting

white cake mix

white chocolate chips

Breads

baguette

brioche bread

ciabatta rolls

croissants

fresh bread crumbs

French bread

Italian bread

Italian bread crumbs

multigrain bread

pita bread

tortillas

whole-wheat bread

Canned Fruit & Juice

cranberry sauce, whole berry and jellied

crushed pineapple

guava juice

Mandarin oranges

mango nectar

pear halves

pomegranate juice

pumpkin purée

raspberry agave nectar

Cheese

blue

Brie cheese round

Camembert

Cheddar

Colby-Jack

cottage

cream cheese, regular and whipped

feta

fontina

fresh mozzarella

garlic spreadable cheese

goat

Gorgonzola

Gruyère

mascarpone

mozzarella, shredded

Parmesan, shredded

queso fresco

Romano, shredded

ricotta

Swiss, slices and shredded

Dairy Section

butter, salted and unsalted

buttermilk

crème fraîche

crescent dinner rolls

eggs

Greek yogurt

Greek yogurt with strawberries

heavy cream

milk, 2%, whole

refrigerated sugar cookie dough

sour cream

whipped cream

Fresh Herbs

basil

chives

cilantro

dill

mint

parsley

rosemary

sage

thyme

Fresh Produce

apples

arugula

asparagus

avocado

baby carrots

bananas

bell peppers

blueberries

broccoli

Broccolini

cabbage

carrots

cauliflower

celery

cherries

corn

cucumber

eggplant

Pantry List

Fresh Produce (cont.)

endive

escarole

fennel bulbs

frisée

garlic

grape tomatoes

grapes, red seedless

grapefruit

green onions

haricots vert

jalapeño pepper

leeks

lemons

lettuce

limes

onions

oranges

peaches

pears

pineapple

potatoes

radicchio

raspberries

red onions

salad greens

salsa

sauerkraut

shallots

Spanish onions

spinach

strawberries

tomatoes, regular and cherry

yellow squash

zucchini

Frozen Foods

baby peas

blueberries

cavatelli

cheese-filled ravioli

chocolate mint chip ice cream

corn

French fries

ice cream sandwiches

meatballs

mini meatballs

peaspie pastry

pink daiquiri mix

potato gnocchi

puff pastry sheets

puff pastry shells

raspberries

ricotta cavatelli

rocky road ice cream

shrimp

sliced strawberries

snow peas

spinach, chopped

vanilla ice cream

whipped topping

Meats, Poultry & Fish

bacon

beef strip steaks

canned tuna

chicken breasts, boneless

chicken drummettes

chicken sausages

chicken thighs

chorizo

cooked chicken

Cornish game hens

filet mignon steak

ground beef

ham hocks

ham steak

loin pork chops

lump crabmeat

meatloaf mix

pancetta

pepperoni

pork tenderloin

prosciutto

salmon

sea scallops

shrimp

sweet Italian sausage

tilapia fillets

white fish fillets

Nuts

almonds, sliced, slivered

macadamia nuts

peanuts

pecans

walnuts

Other

Alfredo sauce

almond paste

apple butter

apple cider vinegar

apricot syrup

artichokes

au jus gravy mix

bacon bits

balsamic vinegar

black beans

blue cheese salad dressing

cannellini beans

capers

caramel sauce

champagne vinegar

chickpeas

chili seasoning mix

Grandpa Misilli (Nonno) in his vineyard in Italy

Pantry List

Other (cont.)

chipotle pepppers in adobo sauce

chocolate hazelnut spread

coconut milk

croutons

crushed tomatoes

Dijon mustard

dried split peas

espresso powder

evaporated milk

farina

fig jam

French fried onions

graham cracker pie crust

green hot pepper sauce

honey

honey mustard

hot fudge sauce

Indian relish

Italian bread crumbs

Italian dressing

Junior Mints

ketchup

kidney bean

lemon curd

lemon-lime soda

lemon vinaigrette

lentils

mashed potato flakes

marinara pasta sauce

mayonnaise

mint Oreo cookies

molasses

mustard, whole grain

oat flakes cereal

olive oil

olive tapenade

olives, black, cured

mango purée

panko bread crumbs

pasteurized cheese product

peanut oil

pepitos

pesto

pine nuts

phyllo cups

quick-cooking oats

ranch dressing

raspberry jam

red wine vinaigrette

red wine vinegar

roasted red peppers

salsa

sesame oil

soy sauce

sun-dried tomatoes

sunflower seeds

tahini

tomato paste

tomatoes, diced, petite diced

water chestnuts

white beans

wonton wrappers

Pasta, Rice, Grains & Noodles

angel hair pasta, refrigerated

Arborio rice

cheese tortellini, refrigerated

couscous

egg noodles

farro

fettuccine

lasagna noodles

long-grain and wild rice

orzo

quinoa

rigatoni

white rice

ziti

Soups & Soup Mixes

beef broth

beef stock

Cheddar cheese soup

chicken broth, regular and low sodium

chicken stock

dry onion soup mix

orange tomato soup

spring vegetable soup mix

vegetable stock

Spices, Seasonings & Flavorings

allspice

cardamom

cayenne pepper

cinnamon

cinnamon stick

cloves, ground

crystallized ginger

cumin

dill

garlic powder

ginger

ground red pepper

herbes de Provence

hot pepper sauce

nutmeg

Old Bay Seasoning

onion powder

oregano

paprika, regular and smoked

pepper

pumpkin pie spice

red pepper flakes

sage

salt

star anise

taco seasoning mix

vanilla extract

white pepper

Wine & Spirits

amaretto liqueur

Cabernet Sauvignon

champagne

coconut-flavored rum

cognac

dark rum

dry red wine

Frangelica

ginger ale

Kahlùa

lime-flavored beer

Madeira wine

pinot grigio

sherry

tequila

white wine

Artichoke, Spinach and Sun-Dried
Tomato Swirls

Spring

PREP	COOK	SERVES
20 min	12 min	4

Artichoke, Spinach and Sun-Dried Tomato Swirls

Shopping List

1 teaspoon butter

1 cup baby spinach, chopped

½ cup whole canned artichoke hearts, drained and chopped

¼ cup sun-dried tomatoes, chopped

½ (17.3-ounce) package puff pastry sheets (1 sheet), thawed

2 tablespoons grated Parmesan cheese

1 egg, beaten with 1 teaspoon water

Tip

These can be made ahead and frozen for up to a month.

STEP 1 Preheat oven to 400°. Line a cookie sheet with parchment paper or lightly spray with cooking spray.

STEP 2 Melt butter over medium-high heat in a small sauté pan. Add spinach and cook for 2 minutes. Transfer to a bowl and stir in artichoke hearts and tomatoes.

STEP 3 Unroll pastry dough sheet on a floured work surface. Roll pastry dough into a 14x11-inch rectangle.

STEP 4 Sprinkle dough with cheese.

STEP 5 Spread spinach mixture on top of cheese, and leave a ½-inch border along the edge of the dough.

STEP 6 Starting at the edge nearest you, tightly roll dough into a log. Trim uneven edges with a sharp knife, and brush egg mixture on top and sides of dough. Pinch ends to seal. Cut log crosswise into ½-inch-thick slices, making 16 pieces. Set slices cut side down 1½ inches apart on cookie sheet.

STEP 7 Bake for 12 minutes or until golden. Remove from cookie sheet, and cool on wire rack for 10 minutes.

notes:

PREP	COOK	SERVES
25 min	15 min	6

Asparagus Rolls

STEP 1 Preheat oven to 400°. Line a cookie sheet with parchment paper, or lightly spray with cooking spray.

STEP 2 Unroll pastry dough sheet on a lightly floured work surface. Roll dough into a 14x11-inch rectangle. Trim dough, if necessary, for a clean edge. Cut dough into 3 crosswise pieces, each measuring approximately 4½x11 inches. Cut each piece into 6 strips approximately 2x4½ inches each, yielding 18 strips.

STEP 3 Sprinkle dough strips with cayenne pepper.

STEP 4 Combine Gruyère and blue cheese. Sprinkle 1 teaspoon cheese mixture on each dough strip.

STEP 5 Place an asparagus spear on top of each dough strip lengthwise, and tightly roll each one (tip of asparagus should be visible). Place pastries seam side down on prepared cookie sheet, and brush with egg mixture.

STEP 6 Bake for 15 minutes at 400° or until golden.

Shopping List

½ (17.3-ounce) package puff pastry sheets (1 sheet), thawed

Cayenne pepper as needed

¼ cup grated Gruyère cheese

¼ cup crumbled blue cheese

18 thin asparagus spears, trimmed to 5-inch lengths

1 egg, beaten with 1 teaspoon water

Tip

These rolls can be assembled ahead and refrigerated.

notes:

PREP	COOK	SERVES
10 min	10 min	4

Roasted Asparagus with Goat Cheese and Citrus Dressing

Shopping List

1 pound asparagus spears, trimmed

1 tablespoon olive oil

Juice and zest of 1 lemon

Salt and pepper to taste

½ cup goat cheese, crumbled

 1 Preheat oven to 400°. Place asparagus in an oven-proof gratin dish. Drizzle with oil, lemon juice and zest, season with salt and pepper, and crumble cheese on top.

 2 Roast in the oven for 8–10 minutes or until cheese is lightly golden, and asparagus is tender.

notes:

Tip

Feta cheese can be substituted for goat cheese, if you prefer.

Roasted Asparagus with Goat
Cheese and Citrus Dressing

SPRING

PREP	SERVES
15 min	4

Olive Tapenade

Shopping List

1 cup mixed pitted olives

¼ cup packed cilantro leaves

1 tablespoon toasted pine nuts

2 teaspoons capers, rinsed and drained

1 small clove garlic, peeled

½ teaspoon lemon zest

 STEP 1 Add olives, cilantro, pine nuts, capers, garlic and zest to a food processor bowl fitted with a metal blade. Pulse until medium chopped, about 20 times.

 STEP 2 Transfer to a small bowl, and mix well.

 **MarkCharles Says:**

Mix a little Olive Tapenade with some mayonnaise for a terrific sandwich spread.

 Tip

This thick olive paste is great on toasted garlic bread.

notes:

Spring

PREP	COOK	SERVES
25 min	20 min	8

Leek, Prosciutto and Fontina Tarts

STEP 1 Preheat oven to 400°. Place phyllo cups inside mini muffin pan cups.

STEP 2 Place butter in a medium sauté pan over medium heat. Add leek. Cook over low heat for 2 minutes or until soft and beginning to brown. Set aside to cool.

STEP 3 In a small bowl, combine leek, egg, heavy cream, prosciutto, fontina and dressing.

STEP 4 Spoon 1 heaping teaspoon leek custard mixture into each phyllo cup. With a knife, make a channel around edges of filling.

STEP 5 Bake for 12–15 minutes at 400° or until set and lightly browned. Cool slightly, and serve.

Shopping List

2 (15-count) packages phyllo cups

2 teaspoons butter

½ cup finely chopped leek, white and pale green parts

1 large egg, beaten

⅓ cup heavy cream

⅓ cup chopped prosciutto

⅓ cup grated fontina cheese

⅓ cup blue cheese salad dressing

notes:

Tip

Substitute cooked ham for prosciutto, if desired.

PREP
30 min

SERVES
6

Southwestern Chicken Salad with Grapes and Walnuts in Mini Pitas

Shopping List

1½ cups shredded rotisserie chicken

½ cup finely chopped red grapes

⅓ cup finely chopped red bell pepper

¼ cup chopped walnuts, toasted

2 tablespoons finely chopped green onions, white and pale green parts, trimmed

2 teaspoons chopped cilantro leaves

1½ teaspoons red wine vinegar

½ teaspoon Dijon mustard

½ teaspoon chipotle chili powder

3 tablespoons canola oil

Salt and freshly ground black pepper to taste

12 mini pitas, sliced in half and lightly toasted

STEP 1 Combine chicken, grapes, red pepper, walnuts, green onions and cilantro in a medium bowl.

STEP 2 Combine vinegar, mustard and chili powder in a small bowl. Slowly whisk in the oil until emulsified. Season with salt and pepper.

STEP 3 Pour vinegar mixture over chicken mixture and toss to combine.

STEP 4 Spoon 1 tablespoon chicken salad into each pita half and serve.

notes:

Tip

Substitute corn or black beans for the red bell pepper.

Spring

PREP 15 min   **SERVES** 4

Hummus with Roasted Garlic, Bacon, and Cilantro Oil

STEP 1 Put the olive oil and cilantro in a food processor fitted with a steel blade, and pulse until smooth. Reserve 3 tablespoons cilantro-flavored oil.

STEP 2 Place garlic, lemon juice, chickpeas, tahini, cumin and bacon in a food processor fitted with a steel blade. Purée until all the ingredients are combined and mixture is smooth. Season with salt and pepper.

STEP 3 Transfer mixture to a serving bowl. Taste and adjust seasonings, if desired. Add additional lemon juice, if needed.

STEP 4 Serve hummus with remaining cilantro oil drizzled on top and toasted pita chips.

Shopping List

- ½ cup extra virgin olive oil
- ¼ cup packed cilantro leaves
- 6 garlic cloves, roasted
- ¼ cup fresh lemon juice
- 1 (15½-ounce) can chickpeas, drained and rinsed
- 2 tablespoons tahini
- 1 tablespoon ground cumin
- 4 strips cooked bacon, crumbled
- Salt and freshly ground black pepper to taste

Tip

Tahini is sesame-seed paste, and is found in the international section of the grocery store.

PREP	COOK	SERVES
10 min	40 min	4 -main course 8 -side dish

SPRING

Baked Risotto with Chicken, Cheese, Asparagus, Bacon and Leeks

Shopping List

1 tablespoon olive oil

1½ cups Arborio rice

5 cups simmering chicken stock, divided

½ cup dry white wine

1½ cups diced cooked chicken

¼ pound asparagus spears, cut on the diagonal into 1-inch pieces (about 1 cup)

1 leek, white and light green part only, cut in half lengthwise, thinly sliced (about 1 cup)

1 cup shredded Parmesan cheese

4 slices bacon, cooked and diced (about ½ cup)

Salt and pepper to taste

STEP 1 Preheat oven to 400°. Place the oil, rice and 4 cups of the heated chicken stock in a dutch oven or 4-quart oven-proof saucepan. Stir, and bake uncovered for 30 minutes, or until most of the liquid is absorbed. Remove from the oven, and place the pan over a low heat.

STEP 2 Add the remaining cup of stock, wine, chicken, asparagus, leek, cheese, and bacon, stirring for 3–5 minutes or until the rice is thick and creamy. Season with salt and pepper to taste.

MarkCharles Says:
Baking this risotto for the first 30 minutes cuts way down on the need to stir.

Tip
Use leftover chicken from a roasted chicken.

notes:

PREP	COOK	SERVES
10 min	40 min	8

Crab and Spring Pea Risotto

STEP 1 Heat oil in a large, heavy-bottomed saucepan. Add onion and garlic, and sauté for 2–3 minutes. Add wine.

STEP 2 Add rice to the pan. Add the stock, 1 cup at a time, stirring and only adding more when the liquid has been absorbed. Repeat the process, stirring constantly to prevent scorching.

STEP 3 Continue adding the stock until the rice grains are tender, but still al dente. After the last of the stock has been absorbed, stir in the crabmeat, peas and cheese. Season with salt and pepper.

notes:

Shopping List

1 tablespoon olive oil

1 small onion, minced (about ½ cup)

1 clove garlic, minced

½ cup dry white wine

1½ cups Arborio rice

5 cups simmering chicken stock

2 (6-ounce) cans fancy lump crabmeat, drained and cleaned (1½ cups)

1½ cups baby peas, thawed, if frozen

½ cup shredded Parmesan cheese

Kosher salt and pepper to taste

Tip

If you run out of stock before the risotto is done, you can finish cooking with hot water, adding only as needed.

 PREP
5 min

SERVES
6

Bellini Splash with Mango

Shopping List

⅓ cup mango purée

¾ cup mango nectar (6 ounces)

1 (750-milliliter) bottle dry champagne (brut) or sparkling wine, chilled

 STEP 1 Place 1 tablespoon mango purée in each of 6 fluted champagne glasses.

STEP 2 Pour 1 ounce mango nectar into each glass.

STEP 3 Holding each champagne glass at an angle, with the tip of the bottle resting just inside the glass, pour in the champagne. Turn glass straight up as it fills.

STEP 4 Serve immediately.

 Tip

Garnish with a fresh mango slice or a sprig of fresh mint.

PREP	COOK	SERVES
25 min	15 min	6

Creamy Fettuccine with Salmon, Sun-Dried Tomatoes, and Baby Peas

STEP 1 Season the salmon with salt and pepper. Heat oil in a skillet, and cook the salmon on both sides until it flakes easily with a fork. Remove the salmon, and flake.

STEP 2 Bring a large pot of water to a boil, and cook the fettuccine. Drain, reserving ½–1 cup of the pasta water.

STEP 3 Add wine to the skillet, and heat to a boil. Add cream, peas, tomatoes and basil. Bring to a boil. Simmer for 2 minutes. Add salmon.

STEP 4 Toss this mixture with the fettuccine, adding reserved pasta water, if necessary. Serve immediately.

Shopping List

1 (¾-pound) salmon fillet

Salt and pepper to taste

1 tablespoon olive oil

1 pound fettuccine

½ cup white wine

1½ cups heavy cream

1 cup baby peas, thawed if frozen

½ cup julienned sun-dried tomatoes

¼ cup julienned basil

notes:

PREP	COOK	SERVES
10 min	40 min	4

Champagne-Roasted Cornish Game Hens

Shopping List

¼ cup olive oil, divided

4 Cornish game hens (about 2 pounds each)

Kosher salt and pepper to taste

1 cup champagne or other sparkling wine or cider

½ cup heavy cream

2 tablespoons chopped parsley

 STEP 1 Preheat oven to 400°. Rub 1 tablespoon oil over each hen. Season with salt and pepper.

 STEP 2 Heat a 12-inch skillet over high heat, and place hens breast-side down in the skillet. Cook until well browned, and then turn over in skillet. Pour champagne over hens, and place the skillet in the oven. Roast for 30–35 minutes at 400°, or until internal temperature of hens is 180°. Baste after 15 minutes.

 STEP 3 Remove hens from skillet, and keep warm. Add cream to skillet, and bring champagne drippings to a boil over medium-high heat to reduce slightly. Stir in herbs.

 STEP 4 Serve each hen with ⅓ cup sauce.

Tip

Serve with mashed potatoes or noodles.

notes:

PREP	COOK	SERVES
20 min	25 min	4

Almond-Crusted Salmon with Thyme and Lemon Butter Sauce

STEP 1 Preheat oven to 400°. Lightly spray a 9x13x2-inch oven-proof casserole with cooking spray, and set aside.

STEP 2 Combine almonds, bread crumbs, garlic, 1 teaspoon zest, thyme, salt and pepper in a small bowl. Stir in oil, and mix well.

STEP 3 Place salmon 2 inches apart in prepared pan. Carefully spoon bread crumb mixture over each fillet, pressing to adhere.

STEP 4 Bake for 18–20 minutes or until salmon flakes easily when tested with fork.

STEP 5 Place wine and lemon juice in a small saucepan. Bring to a boil; cook until reduced by half. Lower heat to medium, and whisk in butter. Add remaining zest. Season with salt and pepper. Spoon sauce over fillets.

Shopping List

¼ cup slivered almonds, chopped

¼ cup packed fresh bread crumbs, made from cubed Portuguese bread, coarsely ground

2 teaspoons minced garlic

2 teaspoons finely grated lemon zest, divided

2 teaspoons crumbled dried thyme

Salt and freshly ground black pepper to taste

2 tablespoons extra virgin olive oil

4 (6-ounce) salmon fillets

½ cup dry white wine

¼ cup lemon juice

4 tablespoons cold butter, cut into 4 pieces

Tip

Add 2 tablespoons rinsed and drained capers to the butter sauce.

SPRING

PREP	COOK	SERVES
10 min	45 min	8

Roasted New Potatoes with Dijon Rosemary Vinaigrette

Shopping List

¼ cup olive oil

Juice and zest of 1 lemon

1 tablespoon Dijon mustard

5 pounds new potatoes, quartered

2 tablespoons chopped rosemary

Kosher salt and pepper to taste

 STEP 1 Heat oven to 400°.

 STEP 2 Whisk olive oil, lemon juice, zest and mustard in a large bowl. Toss with the potatoes and the rosemary. Season well with salt and pepper.

 STEP 3 Transfer to a rimmed baking sheet, and roast 45 minutes or until potatoes are tender. Serve immediately.

notes:

PREP	COOK	SERVES
10 min	20 min	4–6

Chicken with Creamy Sun-Dried Tomato Sauce

STEP 1 Toss the chicken in ¼ cup vinaigrette to coat. Heat oil in a 12-inch skillet, and sauté chicken on both sides until browned. Remove from pan, and keep warm.

STEP 2 Add shallot and garlic. Cook for 3–5 minutes or until softened. Add remaining vinaigrette, and cook an additional minute.

STEP 3 Add cream, tomatoes and pepper flakes; bring to a boil. Reduce heat, and simmer for 5 minutes. Return chicken to the skillet, turning to coat with sauce. Cook an additional 3–5 minutes or until chicken is cooked through. Stir in parsley, season with salt and pepper and serve.

Shopping List

6 boneless chicken breasts (about 1½–2 pounds)

½ cup red wine vinaigrette, divided

1 tablespoon olive oil

1 shallot, minced (about ½ cup)

1 clove garlic, minced

1 cup heavy cream

½ cup julienned sun-dried tomatoes (without oil)

¼ teaspoon red pepper flakes

2 tablespoons chopped parsley

Salt and pepper to taste

notes:

If chicken breasts are very large, cut in half horizontally, or pound to an even thickness for more even cooking.

Mark's Eggs in a Basket

PREP	COOK	SERVES
5 min	5 min	2

Mark's Eggs in a Basket

STEP 1 Cut bread in 8 diagonal slices (1-inch-thick each). With a round metal ring or cookie cutter (about 2 inches across), cut a hole in the center of each slice. Save bread from holes.

STEP 2 Heat a nonstick griddle. Brush with about half the butter, and immediately place 2 slices of the bread and holes on the griddle. Crack open an egg into each hole, and season with salt and pepper. Brush the top of the bread with more butter.

STEP 3 After 1 minute, flip the bread, and season with salt and pepper.

STEP 4 Cook for another minute or 2 (depending on preferred doneness).

STEP 5 Dress the arugula or other greens with the vinaigrette, and place on a platter.

STEP 6 Place eggs and toast on bed of arugula or other greens. Top with shaved Parmesan. Serve immediately along with the toasted bread from the holes.

Shopping List

- 1 loaf Italian bread or sourdough bread, at least 2½ inches in diameter
- 4 tablespoons butter, melted, divided
- 4 large eggs
- Salt and pepper to taste
- 8 ounces arugula or mixed baby greens
- ¼ cup lemon vinaigrette
- ¼ cup shaved Parmesan cheese

notes:

PREP	COOK	SERVES
20 min	15 min	4

Deviled Eggs with Herbed Bread Crumbs

Shopping List

6 large eggs

¼ cup finely ground fresh bread crumbs

1 teaspoon finely chopped parsley

3 tablespoons mayonnaise

1½ teaspoons Dijon mustard

2 teaspoons hot sauce

1½ teaspoons Indian relish

Salt and cayenne pepper to taste

Tip

Slice a tiny piece of egg white from the bottom of each egg half so eggs will sit firmly.

STEP 1 Place eggs in a single layer in a saucepan. Cover with 1 inch of water, and bring to a boil. Cover, and cook over medium heat for 12 minutes. Turn off heat, and drain. Run under cold water, and let eggs sit in cold water until cool.

STEP 2 Place bread crumbs in a small nonstick pan. Cook over medium heat for 3 minutes or until browned, stirring frequently. Remove from heat, and transfer to a small bowl to cool slightly. Stir in parsley, and set aside as a garnish.

STEP 3 Peel eggs, and cut in half lengthwise with a sharp knife dipped in cold water. Remove yolks, and purée in a food processor. Add mayonnaise, mustard, hot sauce, relish, salt and pepper.

STEP 4 Transfer egg mixture into a small zip-top bag, and snip ¼ inch off the bottom corner. Pipe filling into each egg half.

STEP 5 Decorate the eggs with bread crumbs.

notes:

PREP	COOK	SERVES
10 min	10 min	12

Huevos Rancheros Cupcakes

STEP 1 Preheat oven to 350°.

STEP 2 Spray a muffin pan with cooking spray. Carefully line each muffin pan cup with a tortilla, folding to fit. If using bacon, crumble and add inside the tortilla.

STEP 3 Break 1 egg into each tortilla. Bake 10–12 minutes or until whites look set. Remove from oven, and sprinkle each with a slice of crumbled bacon, if desired, and a tablespoon of cheese.

STEP 4 Top each with 2 tablespoons salsa, and sprinkle with cilantro.

Shopping List

12 (6-inch) flour tortillas

12 slices cooked bacon (optional)

12 eggs

¾ cup crumbled queso fresco or shredded Cheddar cheese

1½ cups prepared salsa

½ cup chopped cilantro

MarkCharles Says:

How fun to have a "cupcake" to spice up breakfast!

Tip

If 6-inch tortillas are hard to find, use 8-inch, and trim with scissors.

notes:

Fig and Camembert Ravioli with
Honey Balsamic Glaze

PREP	COOK	SERVES
20 min	10 min	4

Fig and Camembert Ravioli with Honey Balsamic Glaze

STEP 1 Place 4 wonton wrappers at a time on a cutting board. Place 1 piece of cheese and ¼ teaspoon jam on the lower corner of each. Brush edges with egg mixture. Fold the wrappers in half diagonally to seal each ravioli. Place on a floured baking sheet, and cover with a clean towel while assembling the rest. Repeat with remaining wonton wrappers, cheese and jam.

STEP 2 Put vinegar in a small saucepan, and simmer until reduced in half, about 5 minutes. Stir in honey, then add half the butter and the broth, whisking to blend. Simmer while cooking the ravioli.

STEP 3 In a large pot, bring 4 quarts of salted water to a boil. Stir in oil. Carefully add the ravioli 3 or 4 at a time to the pot to keep them from crowding and sticking. Cook for 2–3 minutes or until tender.

STEP 4 Using a slotted spoon, carefully remove the ravioli, toss them in the remaining melted butter and place on serving plates. Keep warm. Drizzle glaze over ravioli, and sprinkle with basil. Serve immediately.

Shopping List

32 wonton wrappers

8 ounces Camembert cheese, cut into 32 pieces (each ¼ inch thick and ¾ inch square)

½ cup fig jam

1 egg, beaten with 1 teaspoon water

1 (4-ounce) stick butter, melted, divided

¼ cup balsamic vinegar

1 tablespoon honey

½ cup chicken broth or water

Salt to taste

4 quarts water

1 tablespoon olive oil

2 tablespoons julienned basil

notes:

PREP	COOK	SERVES
10 min	20 min	6

Fresh Peas with Bacon and Caramelized Onions

Shopping List

8 slices bacon, chopped

1 medium onion, thinly sliced

½ teaspoon salt

2 teaspoons sugar

3 cups fresh peas

¾ cup vegetable or chicken broth

STEP 1 Cook bacon in 12-inch skillet over medium heat until crisp; remove bacon, and set aside. Pour off all but 2 tablespoons drippings.

STEP 2 Add onion and salt. Cook over medium heat for 10 minutes, stirring occasionally, until tender and golden. Add sugar, and cook for 1 minute. Stir in peas and broth, and bring to a boil. Simmer over medium heat 5 minutes or until peas are tender. Stir in bacon, and serve.

notes:

Frozen peas work just as well; no need to thaw, just cook as directed.

Fresh Peas with Bacon and Caramelized Onions

PREP	COOK	SERVES
10 min	10 min	4

Garlic Shrimp and Pasta

Shopping List

2 (9-ounce) packages refrigerated fresh angel hair pasta

4 tablespoons olive oil

4 tablespoons butter

3 garlic cloves, minced

1½ pounds raw shrimp, cleaned, tails removed

¾ cup fresh lemon juice

2 tablespoons each: chopped fresh parsley, chives, basil, and thyme

Salt and pepper to taste

Grated Parmesan cheese

STEP 1 Cook the pasta in a large pot of boiling water until al dente.

STEP 2 Heat oil and butter in a large skillet, and sauté garlic and shrimp until the shrimp turn pink.

STEP 3 Drain pasta.

STEP 4 Add lemon juice and herbs to shrimp, and toss gently with pasta. Season with salt and pepper. Serve with cheese.

notes:

Spring Greens with Avocado Lime Dressing

STEP 1 Add avocado, buttermilk, lime juice, cilantro and salt to food processor bowl fitted with a metal blade. Process until smooth. Add additional buttermilk, if needed, for desired consistency.

STEP 2 Toss dressing with salad greens and tomatoes. Sprinkle with pepitos and queso fresco.

Shopping List

1 ripe avocado, halved, pit removed

½ cup buttermilk

2 tablespoons lime juice

5 sprigs fresh cilantro (about 1 tablespoon, chopped)

½ teaspoon salt

1 (7-ounce) package mesclun salad greens (about 8 cups)

1 cup grape tomatoes, halved

3 tablespoons pepitos (pumpkin seeds)

¼ cup crumbled queso fresco

notes:

For a kicked-up version, add ¼ teaspoon chipotle chili powder. Top with grilled shrimp or chicken for a main-dish salad.

PREP
10 min

COOK
20 min

SERVES
4

Lemon and Asparagus Tart

Shopping List

½ (17.3-ounce) package puff
  pastry sheets (1 sheet), thawed

¾ cup shredded fontina cheese,
  divided

1 pound thin asparagus spears,
  trimmed

1½ teaspoons olive oil

½ teaspoon cracked black pepper

Juice and zest of 1 lemon

 1 Heat oven to 400°. Unfold pastry sheet onto a parchment-lined baking sheet. Using a sharp knife, score a line ½ inch inside the edge of the pastry sheet to form a border. Prick the inside of the pastry sheet with a fork.

 3 Sprinkle half the cheese on the pastry sheet inside the border. Place asparagus in a large bowl, and toss with oil, pepper, lemon juice and zest. Arrange asparagus on top of the cheese, alternating points and ends, stacking to fit, if needed.

 4 Bake for 20 minutes or until the crust is golden brown. Sprinkle with the remaining cheese.

If using larger spears, slice them in half lengthwise before proceeding.

notes:

Spring

PREP	COOK	SERVES
20 min	20-25 min	8

Strawberry Lemon-Lime Soda Cake

STEP 1 Preheat oven to 350°. Spray sides and bottom of 13x9x2-inch metal or glass pan, and flour lightly.

STEP 2 Place cake mix, egg whites, soda and purée in a large bowl. Beat at low speed until moistened. Raise speed to medium, and beat for 2 minutes. Pour batter into prepared pan. Bake for 20–25 minutes or until toothpick inserted in center comes out clean.

STEP 3 Cool cake in pan for 15 minutes. Invert onto cake rack, and cool completely before frosting.

STEP 4 Remove frosting from container, and place in a bowl. Stir in orange extract. Decorate cake with frosting.

Shopping List

1 (18¼-ounce) box white cake mix

3 large egg whites

¾ cup lemon-lime soda

½ cup strawberry purée

1 (12-ounce) can whipped white frosting

1 teaspoon orange extract

MarkCharles Says:

Play "guess the ingredients" with your family when you serve this great little cake!

Tip

Garnish with sliced fresh strawberries.

notes:

PREP
15 min

SERVES
6

Sweet Strawberry and Yogurt Pie

Shopping List

12 ounces whole frozen strawberries with no sugar added,
thawed

2 (5.3-ounce) containers Greek
yogurt with strawberries

2 cups low-calorie frozen whipped
topping, thawed

1 (9-inch) prepared graham-
cracker pie crust

STEP 1 Place strawberries in a food processor bowl fitted with a steel blade, and process until puréed. Transfer to a large bowl.

STEP 2 Add yogurt and whipped topping to strawberry purée. Stir until completely mixed.

STEP 3 Using a rubber spatula, pour yogurt mixture into pie crust.

STEP 4 Place pie in freezer, and freeze for 3–4 hours or over-night. Remove pie to room temperature for 10 min-utes before serving.

Tip

Decorate top with
sliced fresh
strawberries.

Leo and Marli with Parfait the dog

PREP	COOK	SERVES
15 min	12 min	4

Raspberry Linzer Rounds

STEP 1 Preheat oven to 350°.

STEP 2 Cut dough into 24 (¼-inch) slices, and place half of the cookie rounds on an ungreased cookie sheet. Space about 2 inches apart. Using a 1-inch diameter cookie cutter, cut out the centers of half the rounds. Place the remaining cookies on another ungreased cookie sheet, spaced about 2 inches apart.

STEP 3 Bake cookies for 12 minutes or until edges are a light golden color. Cool for several minutes, and remove from cookie sheets.

STEP 4 When cookies are cool, spread 1 tablespoon jam on each whole cookie. Gently press the cut-out cookie on top.

STEP 5 Dust cookies generously with confectioners' sugar.

Shopping List

1 (15½-ounce) roll refrigerated sugar cookie dough

¾ cup raspberry jam

Confectioners' sugar, as needed

Tip

Sprinkle toasted, chopped nuts on top of jam. Use a small offset spatula to easily spread the jam.

notes:

Grapefruit and Orange Salsa

Summer

PREP	SERVES
25 min	8

Grapefruit and Orange Salsa

Shopping List

1 medium grapefruit, sectioned, seeded and coarsely chopped, juice reserved (1 cup)

1 large orange, sectioned, seeded and coarsely chopped, juice reserved (1 cup)

1 medium tomato, chopped (1 cup)

1 small red bell pepper, seeded and chopped (1 cup)

½ cup chopped red onion

1 jalapeño pepper, seeded and chopped

2 tablespoons chopped fresh cilantro

1 tablespoon lime juice

2 teaspoons sugar

½ teaspoon salt

 STEP 1 Combine grapefruit, orange, tomato, red pepper, onion, and jalapeño in a medium bowl. Combine cilantro, lime juice, sugar and salt in a small bowl, and stir until sugar is dissolved. Add cilantro mixture to grapefruit mixture. Stir to mix well.

 STEP 2 Serve with blue corn tortilla chips.

notes:

Tip

This is delicious served over steak, chicken, fish or baked potatoes. It's also a great salsa for fish tacos.

PREP	COOK	SERVES
15 min	25 min	6

Chorizo and Shrimp en Croûte

STEP 1 Add chorizo to a large nonstick skillet. Cook over medium heat for 8 minutes or until well browned. Remove, and set aside.

STEP 2 Add oil to skillet. Add onion and salt. Cook over medium heat for 5 minutes or until onion is tender. Add garlic, and cook for 1 minute. Add shrimp, and continue to cook over medium heat for 3 minutes or until shrimp are almost done.

STEP 3 Return chorizo to skillet. Add wine, paprika, and cilantro. Bring to a boil, and simmer over medium heat for 5 minutes or until shrimp are just cooked. Serve over baked puff pastry shells.

Shopping List

¾ pound chorizo, thinly sliced on the diagonal

1 tablespoon olive oil

1 large onion, thinly sliced

½ teaspoon salt

1 tablespoon minced garlic

1 pound large shrimp, peeled and deveined

¾ cup dry white wine

2 teaspoons paprika

2 tablespoons minced cilantro or parsley

1 (10-ounce) package puff pastry shells, prepared according to package directions

SUMMER

MarkCharles Says:

"En Croûte" is French and means wrapped in pastry, and this recipe gives you the same great effect, but is much easier to do."

notes:

Tip

This shortcut recipe directs you to serve the shrimp and chorizo over the puff pastry, eliminating the fussy step of wrapping.

PREP	COOK	SERVES
1 hour	15 min	4

SUMMER

Chipotle Cherry Pork Salad

Shopping List

¼ cup lime juice

1 chipotle in adobo, minced

½ cup olive oil

1 pork tenderloin, butterflied

3 tablespoons chopped cilantro

2 cups farro, quinoa or couscous, cooked just until tender

½ cup dried cherries, softened

1 cup diced red or yellow bell peppers

½ cup minced green onions

Salt to taste

STEP 1 Combine lime juice and chipotle in a small bowl. Slowly whisk in oil. Pour ⅓ cup mixture over pork; reserve remaining mixture. Marinate pork 45–60 minutes.

STEP 2 Grill pork 10–12 minutes or until cooked through. Let stand 15 minutes.

STEP 3 Combine remaining chipotle mixture with cilantro, farro, cherries, peppers and green onions. Toss well to coat. Slice pork, and serve over the farro. Season with salt to taste.

Tip

Replace pork with chicken. You can also serve the meat over greens as well as your choice of grain.

PREP	COOK	SERVES
15 min	20 min	4

Cavatelli with Sausage and Broccolini®

STEP 1 Heat 1 tablespoon oil in a 12-inch skillet. Add sausage, and cook until browned. Remove from skillet with slotted spoon.

STEP 2 Add onion to skillet and cook for 4 minutes or until onion starts to brown, stirring occasionally. Add garlic, and cook for 30 seconds or until fragrant. Add Broccolini, broth, tomatoes and pepper flakes, and bring to a boil.

STEP 3 Reduce heat, and simmer, covered, for 4 minutes or until Broccolini is tender. Add cavatelli, reserved pasta water and sausage. Toss to coat, and cook 1 minute.

STEP 4 Sprinkle with cheese. Just before serving, drizzle with remaining 2 tablespoons oil. Season with salt and black pepper, and garnish with parsley.

notes:

Shopping List

3 tablespoons extra virgin olive oil, divided

1 pound sweet Italian sausage, removed from casings and crumbled (not too small)

1 cup finely chopped onion

3 garlic cloves, finely chopped

1 bunch Broccolini, trimmed

2 cups chicken broth

⅓ cup oil-packed, sun-dried tomatoes, thinly sliced

⅛ teaspoon red pepper flakes

1 (13-ounce) bag frozen ricotta cavatelli, cooked according to package directions, reserving ¼ cup pasta water

¼ cup shredded Parmesan cheese

Salt and black pepper to taste

Fresh chopped parsley for garnish

Tip

If Broccolini is unavailable, trim a small head of broccoli into thin spears.

Summer

Kim and Jeff's Peppered Pork Medallions with Lemon and Capers

Shopping List

1 tablespoon coarsely ground black pepper

1 pound pork tenderloin, cut into 12 (1-inch-thick) medallions

1 tablespoon oil

4 tablespoons butter, divided

Kosher salt to taste

¼ cup minced shallots

¼ cup cognac

1 cup chicken stock or broth

¼ cup fresh lemon juice

2 tablespoons capers, drained

1 lemon, peeled and sectioned, membranes and seeds removed

Fresh chives or parsley, chopped (optional)

STEP 1 Press pepper onto both sides of pork.

STEP 2 Heat oil and 1 tablespoon butter in large, heavy skillet over medium heat. Sprinkle pork with salt. Cook until just cooked through, about 4 minutes per side. Transfer pork to heat-resistant plate, and keep warm in 300° oven.

STEP 3 Remove skillet drippings. Add shallots, and cook for 1–2 minutes. Remove skillet from heat. Deglaze skillet with cognac. Add stock and lemon juice to skillet. Return to heat, and simmer sauce until reduced to ½ cup, 4–5 minutes.

STEP 4 Remove skillet from heat. Whisk in remaining 3 tablespoons butter. Add capers, lemon segments and fresh herbs, if desired; add pork to coat with sauce.

Tip

Serve pork over pasta or rice, or with green beans and potatoes.

PREP	COOK	SERVES
20 min	35 min	6

Fiesta Fish Tacos

Shopping List

For Aïoli Cream:

⅓ cup mayonnaise

2 tablespoons sour cream or Greek yogurt

4 green onions, trimmed and thinly sliced

¼ cup chopped fresh cilantro

Juice and zest of 1 lemon

1 tablespoon Old Bay Seasoning®

Hot pepper sauce

For Tacos:

1¼ pounds white fish fillets (red snapper, cod, haddock or tilapia)

2 tablespoons olive oil

1 tablespoon lemon juice

2 teaspoons Old Bay Seasoning

1 teaspoon smoked paprika

6 (8-inch) tortillas

2 cups shredded cabbage

2 cups diced tomatoes

STEP 1 Preheat oven to 425°.

STEP 2 Combine mayonnaise, sour cream, onions, cilantro, lemon juice and zest, seasoning and pepper sauce in a bowl; set aside.

STEP 3 Brush fish with oil, and sprinkle with lemon juice. Place on a baking sheet. Combine seasoning and paprika in a small bowl, and sprinkle over both sides of fish. Bake at 425° for 8–10 minutes or until fish flakes easily with a fork, or until desired degree of doneness.

STEP 4 Break fish apart with a fork. Heat tortillas according to package directions. Divide fish evenly among tortillas, and top with cabbage, tomatoes and Aïoli Cream. Serve immediately.

Tip

Use shrimp, if preferred. Hard corn taco shells can be used in place of tortillas. Fish can be served on a salad instead of in taco shells.

PREP	COOK	SERVES
15 min	15 min	4

Mediterranean Couscous

STEP 1 Heat 2 tablespoons oil in 4-quart saucepan over medium-high heat. Cook onion for 4 minutes or until starting to brown, stirring occasionally. Add zucchini, and cook for 2 minutes or until starting to soften, stirring occasionally. Add garlic, and cook for 1 minute or until fragrant. Stir in lemon juice and chicken broth, and bring to a boil.

STEP 2 Stir in couscous, tomatoes, cheese, oregano, salt and pepper. Cover, and let stand 5 minutes.

STEP 3 Meanwhile, coat 4 (1-cup) ramekins, bowls, or tea cups with remaining oil. Evenly place arugula in bottoms of ramekins. Top evenly with warm couscous mixture, pressing down firmly to compact.

STEP 4 To serve, invert onto dinner plate. Garnish top with arugula leaves, and drizzle with remaining olive oil. May also garnish with lemon wedges, if desired.

Shopping List

3 tablespoons extra virgin olive oil, divided

1 cup finely chopped sweet onion

1 medium zucchini, diced

1 clove garlic, finely chopped

2 teaspoons lemon juice

1 cup chicken broth

¾ cup couscous

1 cup cherry tomatoes, halved

¼ cup shredded Parmesan cheese

1 tablespoon finely chopped fresh oregano or basil

½ teaspoon sea salt

⅛ teaspoon freshly ground black pepper

1 cup baby arugula

1 lemon, cut into wedges (optional)

notes:

Recipe can easily be doubled for a party and served in a large bowl.

Grilled New Potatoes with Spinach
and Warm Bacon Vinaigrette

PREP	COOK	SERVES
20 min	30 min	8

Grilled New Potatoes with Spinach and Warm Bacon Vinaigrette

STEP 1 **Potatoes:** Toss potatoes and onion with olive oil, salt and pepper until well coated. Evenly spread down center of 12x18-inch piece of heavy-duty aluminum foil. Wrap foil loosely around potatoes, sealing edges airtight with double fold. Grill for about 30 minutes, or until potatoes are tender, turning twice.

STEP 2 **Warm Bacon Vinaigrette:** Cook bacon in small sauce-pan until crisp. Remove with slotted spoon; reserve. Add oil, and heat over medium heat. Cook onion for 4 minutes or until golden brown, whisking frequently. Stir in vinegar, broth, mustard, honey, salt and pepper. Simmer for 5 minutes or until slightly reduced, whisking frequently.

STEP 3 Arrange spinach in bottom of salad bowl. Top with hot grilled potatoes, and let stand 5 minutes. Drizzle with vinaigrette, and sprinkle with reserved bacon. Serve warm or at room temperature.

notes:

Shopping List

For Potatoes:

1½ pounds assorted new potatoes, cut into bite-sized chunks

1 cup chopped sweet onion

2 tablespoons extra virgin olive oil

¼ teaspoon salt

⅛ teaspoon freshly ground black pepper

For Warm Bacon Vinaigrette:

6 slices hickory-smoked bacon, chopped

2 tablespoons extra virgin olive oil

4 tablespoons finely chopped sweet onion

4 tablespoons apple cider vinegar

4 tablespoons chicken broth

1 tablespoon whole-grain mustard

1 tablespoon honey

¼ teaspoon salt

⅛ teaspoon freshly ground black pepper

1 (5-ounce) package baby spinach

SUMMER

Tip

Try using "rainbow" new potatoes for a gourmet look.

PREP	COOK	SERVES
30 min	30 min	4

SUMMER

California Ranch Grilled French Fry Salad

Shopping List

1 (28-ounce) bag frozen julienne French fries with sea salt

⅓ cup mayonnaise

⅓ cup buttermilk

⅓ cup sour cream

2 teaspoons minced garlic

1 teaspoon onion powder

2 tablespoons lemon juice

Salt and freshly ground black pepper to taste

4 cups baby salad greens

3 medium tomatoes, cored and chopped (1½ cups)

1 ripe avocado, peeled and chopped (1 cup)

1 bunch green onions, white and green parts, chopped

2 tablespoons chopped chives

STEP 1 Preheat grill to medium heat. Place ⅓ French fries on a perforated pizza pan, or pan designed for cooking vegetables on grill.

STEP 2 Cook fries on covered grill for 8–10 minutes or until golden brown, turning over halfway through cooking time. Repeat twice more with remaining fries.

STEP 3 Combine mayonnaise, buttermilk, sour cream, garlic, onion powder and lemon juice. Season with salt and pepper. Set aside.

STEP 4 Place salad greens on large platter, spreading them out to the sides of the platter. Mound fries on greens. Sprinkle tomatoes and avocado around edges of platter over greens. Spoon dressing over salad. Top with green onions and chives.

notes:

Tip

Add cilantro leaves instead of chives.

PREP
15 min

SERVES
4

Red Grape, Feta and Baby Arugula with Roasted Sunflower Seeds

STEP 1 Whisk oil, lemon juice, vinegar, mustard and honey in small bowl. Season with salt and pepper.

STEP 2 Arrange arugula, grapes and onion on serving platter, and top with feta cheese. Drizzle with dressing, and sprinkle with sunflower seeds.

Shopping List

4 tablespoons extra virgin olive oil

2 tablespoons fresh lemon juice

2 tablespoons apple cider vinegar or white balsamic vinegar

1 tablespoon whole-grain mustard

2 teaspoons honey

Salt and freshly ground black pepper to taste

1 (5-ounce) package baby arugula (2½ cups)

2 cups halved red seedless grapes

¼ cup very thinly sliced red onion

¼ cup crumbled feta cheese

4 tablespoons roasted sunflower seeds

Tip

Evenly divide arugula, grapes, onion and feta cheese on 4 salad plates. Drizzle each with 2 tablespoons dressing and sprinkle each with 1 tablespoon sunflower seeds.

PREP	COOK	SERVES
10 min	25 min	6

SUMMER

BLT and Basil Bites with Caramelized Shallots

Shopping List

1 (9-inch) refrigerated pie crust

8 slices bacon, chopped

6 large shallots, peeled and thinly sliced

½ teaspoon salt

1 large tomato, chopped and drained

½ cup shredded lettuce

2 tablespoons chopped fresh basil

¼ cup mayonnaise

STEP 1 Heat oven to 400°. Spray 24 mini muffin cups with cooking spray.

STEP 2 Remove pie crust from pouch; place flat on a lightly floured cutting board or pastry cloth. With 2½-inch round cutter, cut 12 rounds from each crust. Press 1 round into bottom and up sides of each muffin cup. Prick pastry all over with a fork. Bake 7–9 minutes or until golden. Cool for 5 minutes; remove from pan, and cool completely.

STEP 3 Cook bacon in a large skillet over medium heat until crisp. Remove, and set aside. Pour off all but 2 tablespoons bacon drippings. Add shallots and salt. Cook over medium heat for 10 minutes or until tender and golden, stirring occasionally.

STEP 4 Combine bacon, tomato, lettuce, basil, and mayonnaise.

STEP 5 Fill each pie crust with about 1 teaspoon caramelized shallots, and top with 1 tablespoon bacon mixture.

Tip

For added convenience, use mini phyllo cups instead of the pie crust.

notes:

PREP	COOK	SERVES
15 min	10 min	6

Haricots Vert and Cherry Tomatoes with Minted Crème Fraîche

STEP 1 Blend crème fraîche, mint, milk, sugar, ⅛ teaspoon salt and ⅛ teaspoon pepper in small bowl; set aside.

STEP 2 Arrange cherry tomatoes and arugula in medium bowl. Toss with remaining salt, pepper, olive oil and lemon juice, and set aside.

STEP 3 Blanch or steam green beans until tender-crisp. Top cherry tomatoes and arugula mixture with hot beans. Cover, and let stand 5 minutes.

STEP 4 Uncover, and toss. Arrange bean mixture on platter, and drizzle with minted crème.

Shopping List

- 1 cup crème fraîche or sour cream
- 2 tablespoons chopped fresh mint
- 2 tablespoons milk
- 1 teaspoon sugar
- ¼ teaspoon salt, divided
- ¼ teaspoon ground black pepper, divided
- 10 ounces cherry tomatoes, halved
- 2 cups baby arugula
- 1 tablespoon extra virgin olive oil
- 1 tablespoon fresh lemon juice
- 8 ounces haricots vert or thin green beans, trimmed

MarkCharles Says:

"Haricots Vert" is French for green beans—use the thinnest green beans you can find. Serve them in a saucer to mix it up a bit."

notes:

Tip

Try using yellow and red tomatoes for a color splash! Serve in fancy plastic cups or martini glasses dolloped with crème.

SUMMER

PREP	COOK	SERVES
15 min	10 min	6

Grilled Scallops over Grilled Greens

SUMMER

Shopping List

2 tablespoons smoked paprika

¼ teaspoon cayenne pepper

1½ teaspoons ground mustard

24 sea scallops (dry packed)

Sea salt and cracked black pepper to taste

3 tablespoons olive oil

2 garlic cloves, minced

2 heads radicchio, cut into 6 wedges, core intact

1 head escarole, halved

12 green onions

Juice of 2 lemons

1 lemon, cut into 6 wedges

STEP 1 Mix paprika, cayenne and mustard in a small bowl.

STEP 2 Season scallops with salt and pepper. Rub with spice mixture.

STEP 3 Combine oil, garlic, salt and pepper. Brush leaves of radicchio, escarole and onions with mixture.

STEP 4 Preheat grill. Grill scallops over high heat for about 2 minutes each side. Set aside.

STEP 5 Grill greens until just wilted and caramelized. Grill onions until tender and slightly charred. Lay greens and onions on plate; top with scallops, and drizzle with lemon juice. Serve with lemon wedges.

Tip

Grilled bread is a wonderful accompaniment.

PREP	COOK	SERVES
20 min	20 min	4

Frisée Salad with Egg, Endive and Bacon

STEP 1 Slice bacon into ¼-inch strips. Heat a medium sauté pan over medium-high heat. Add bacon, and cook, stirring often, until crisp. Use a slotted spoon to transfer bacon to a paper-towel-lined plate to drain.

STEP 2 Combine shallot, mustard, vinegar and sugar in small bowl. Add oil in a slow, steady stream, whisking vigorously and continuously, until vinaigrette is creamy and emulsified. Season with salt and pepper. Set aside.

STEP 3 Combine frisée, endive, bacon and croutons in large bowl. Add enough vinaigrette to lightly coat the salad. Season with salt and pepper. Divide salad evenly among salad plates. Top each salad with sliced egg, and serve immediately.

notes:

Shopping List

6 slices thick-cut bacon

1 large shallot, finely chopped

1 teaspoon Dijon mustard

4 tablespoons red wine vinegar

2 teaspoons sugar

4 tablespoons extra virgin olive oil

Salt and freshly ground pepper to taste

1 medium head frisée or mixed greens

2 endive, cut into strips

1 cup croutons

4 large eggs, hard-cooked, peeled and sliced

Tip

If you can't find frisée, substitute arugula, mixed baby greens or baby spinach.

Summer

PREP
20 min

SERVES
6

Chicken and Blueberry Salad with Creamy Lemon Vinaigrette

Shopping List

3 cups diced cooked chicken

1 cup blueberries

1 cup thinly sliced celery

½ cup chopped pecans, toasted

¼ cup olive oil

2 tablespoons mayonnaise

1 tablespoon lemon juice

2 teaspoons fresh thyme, chopped

1 clove garlic, minced

½ teaspoon salt

¼ teaspoon ground black pepper

12 slices multigrain bread

1½ cups baby spinach or arugula

STEP 1 Combine chicken, blueberries, celery and pecans in a large bowl; set aside.

STEP 2 Place oil, mayonnaise, lemon juice, thyme, garlic, salt and pepper in a medium bowl. Mix well with wire whisk. Add to chicken mixture, and toss gently until evenly coated.

STEP 3 Divide mixture among 6 slices bread; top with spinach and remaining bread slices.

MarkCharles Says:

"Create food memories by taking the family blueberry picking, then make this dish together. Pull out your double Old-Fashioned glasses to serve this salad for a change of pace."

Tip

Omit the bread and spinach. Serve the chicken salad with romaine or Boston lettuce leaves to make Chicken and Blueberry Lettuce Wraps.

notes:

PREP	COOK	SERVES
15 min	8 min	6

Broccoli and Yellow Pepper Stir-Fry with Toasted Sesame Seeds

 STEP 1 Combine soy sauce, honey, sherry and ginger in a small bowl; set aside.

 STEP 2 Heat oil in a 12-inch skillet over medium-high heat. Cook peppers and onion for 5 minutes or until starting to brown, stirring occasionally. Add garlic, and cook 30 seconds or until fragrant. Add broccoli, and cook for 2 minutes or until tender, stirring occasionally. Stir in soy sauce mixture, and toss to coat. Sprinkle with sesame seeds and black pepper.

notes:

Shopping List

- 2 tablespoons soy sauce
- 1 tablespoon honey
- 1 tablespoon sherry
- ¼ teaspoon ground ginger
- 2 tablespoons olive or vegetable oil
- 2 large yellow bell peppers, seeded and cut into thin strips
- 1 large sweet onion, sliced
- 1 clove garlic, finely chopped
- 4 cups broccoli florets, steamed or blanched crisp-tender
- 2 teaspoons toasted sesame seeds
- ⅛ teaspoon black pepper

SUMMER

Tip

Substitute black sesame seeds for white, and red or orange bell peppers for yellow.

PREP	SERVES
15 min	4

Mozzarella Seafood Parfaits

SUMMER

Shopping List

½ ball fresh mozzarella in water, diced

3 tablespoons prepared pesto

2 tablespoons red wine vinegar or lemon juice

2 ripe avocados, peeled, seeded and diced

3 ripe Roma tomatoes, diced

1 English cucumber, diced

½ cup cooked lump crabmeat, small shrimp, or diced lobster

Lemon slices and chopped chives

STEP 1 Combine mozzarella, pesto and vinegar, and toss to coat.

STEP 2 In 4 Old-Fashioned glasses, layer avocado, tomato and cucumber. Top with mozzarella. Top with desired shellfish, lemon slice and chopped chives.

MarkCharles Says:

"Get out your margarita or martini glasses, and serve this dish in those to elevate it to celebration status!"

notes:

PREP	COOK	SERVES
20 min	17 min	6

Roasted Corn, Tomato, Avocado and Black Bean Tarts

STEP 1 Preheat oven to 450°. Turn 6-cup muffin pan with regular-size cups upside down. Spray backs of muffin cups with nonstick cooking spray. Using 4-inch round cookie cutter, cut 6 rounds from pie crust. Place dough rounds over backs of muffin cups, pleating dough to fit around cups. Pierce dough several times with fork. Bake 5–10 minutes or until lightly browned. Cool for 5 minutes. Carefully remove tart shells from muffin cups; place open sides up on cooling rack.

STEP 2 Arrange corn on a baking sheet, and toss with ½ teaspoon salt and olive oil. Roast 10 minutes or until corn begins to brown, stirring occasionally. Remove from oven; cool slightly.

STEP 3 Combine roasted corn with tomato, avocado, beans, onion, cilantro, ranch dressing, lime juice, hot sauce, and remaining ½ teaspoon salt in a large bowl. Toss until evenly coated. Divide evenly among tart shells.

Shopping List

1 (9-inch) refrigerated pie crust

1½ cups fresh or frozen corn

1 teaspoon salt, divided

1 teaspoon olive oil

1 large tomato, chopped

1 large ripe avocado, diced

1 cup black beans, rinsed and drained

2 tablespoons chopped red onion

2 tablespoons chopped fresh cilantro

1 tablespoon ranch dressing

1 tablespoon lime juice

1 teaspoon green hot pepper sauce

notes:

Tip

This makes a great first course—or use it to serve 2 as a vegetarian main dish. Make mini tarts by cutting 2 pie crusts into 24 (2½-inch) rounds. Line a mini muffin pan with rounds, and bake at 400° for 7 minutes or until golden.

PREP	COOK	SERVES
15 min	20 min	4

Grilled Sausage and Arugula

Shopping List

- 1 pound seasoned sausage in casing
- 1 (6-ounce) bag baby arugula
- 1 tablespoon Dijon mustard
- 2 tablespoons lemon juice
- ¼ cup olive oil
- ½ cup minced roasted red bell pepper
- 2 tablespoons chopped chives or parsley
- Salt and cracked black pepper to taste
- 4 peaches, cut in quarters, seeded and grilled
- Shaved Parmesan (optional)

STEP 1 Cook sausage according to package directions.

STEP 2 Place arugula in a large bowl.

STEP 3 Combine mustard and lemon juice in a bowl, and slowly whisk in oil. Add red peppers, chives, salt and pepper. Toss half of the mixture with the arugula, and divide among 4 plates; reserve remaining lemon juice mixture.

STEP 4 Place ¼ of the sausage on each plate, and top each with remaining dressing. Top with grilled peaches. Sprinkle with shaved Parmesan, if desired.

Tip

Serve sausage over grilled eggplant, grilled sweet onions, or both.

Leo, Mark and MarkCharles

PREP	COOK	SERVES
20 min	6 min	4

Chicken Paillard

STEP 1 Split and butterfly chicken breasts. Place between sheets of wax paper, and pound to create a thin, large piece.

STEP 2 Combine garlic, mustard, lemon juice, herbs and oil in a large bowl. Mix well. Add chicken, and turn to coat. Let stand 20–25 minutes.

STEP 3 Remove chicken from lemon juice mixture. Set grill at high. Sprinkle chicken with salt and pepper. Grill chicken 3–4 minutes per side or until cooked through. Cool, and serve warm or room temperature over greens with sliced tomatoes.

Shopping List

4 boneless, skinless chicken breast halves

2 garlic cloves, minced

1 tablespoon Dijon mustard

2 tablespoons lemon juice

3 tablespoons fresh chopped herbs (sage, parsley or chives)

2 tablespoons olive oil

Salt and cracked black pepper to taste

Salad greens and sliced tomatoes

SUMMER

MarkCharles Says:

"Use a rolling pin and zip-top bag to pound the chicken into thin pieces to keep things neat and clean. The thinner pieces cook quickly and evenly any time you want to speed things up."

Tip

Slice chicken, and serve in wraps or pasta dishes.

notes:

PREP
10

Rita's Dip

Shopping List

1 cup mayonnaise

1 cup sour cream

1 (.9-ounce) package Knorr® Spring Vegetable Recipe Mix

1 (5-ounce) can solid white tuna, drained

1 (10-ounce) box chopped frozen spinach, thawed and squeezed dry

½ teaspoon dried tarragon

¼ teaspoon Old Bay Seasoning

Salt and pepper to taste

STEP 1 Combine mayonnaise, sour cream, soup mix, tuna, spinach, tarragon, seasoning, salt and pepper in a medium bowl until well mixed.

STEP 2 Cover and refrigerate for at least 1 hour before serving. Serve with your favorite crackers and cut-up vegetables.

PREP	COOK	SERVES
10 min	10 min	4

Margarita Shrimp Sauté

STEP 1 Heat oil in a 10-inch nonstick skillet over medium-high heat. Add the shrimp, and cook for about 5 minutes. Add dressing, and stir to coat shrimp.

STEP 2 Stir in corn, tomatoes, tequila and lime juice. Cook for about 5 minutes more or until shrimp turns pink and flavors are blended.

STEP 3 Stir in the cilantro. Serve over rice or salad greens.

SUMMER

Shopping List

1 tablespoon olive oil

1 pound large frozen shrimp, thawed

½ cup Italian dressing

1 (10-ounce) package frozen whole-kernel corn (1½ cups)

1 (14½-ounce) can diced tomatoes, drained

2 tablespoons tequila

1 tablespoon lime juice

2 tablespoons chopped fresh cilantro leaves

Hot cooked rice or shredded lettuce

notes:

Meme and Mom

PREP	COOK	SERVES
10 min	55 min	12

Summer Harvest Bread Pudding

Shopping List

9 croissants, halved lengthwise

4 cups assorted blueberries, raspberries, and sliced strawberries, divided

6 eggs

2 cups whole milk

1 cup heavy cream

1 cup brown sugar

¼ cup Frangelico® or Grand Marnier®

STEP 1 Preheat oven to 350°. Spray an 8x12-inch baking dish with nonstick cooking spray. Arrange bottom halves of croissants in baking dish, overlapping, if necessary.

STEP 2 Sprinkle 3 cups berries over croissants. Arrange croissant tops over berries, overlapping to fit, if needed. Top with remaining berries.

STEP 3 Combine eggs, milk, cream, sugar, and liqueur, and pour over croissants. Let stand at least 15 minutes for custard mixture to soak into croissants.

STEP 4 Cover with aluminum foil, and bake for 30 minutes; uncover and bake 25 minutes until golden and set.

notes:

 Tip

Try using donuts instead of croissants.

PREP	COOK	SERVES
15 min	10 min	12

Triple Mint Ice Cream Pizza

STEP 1 Preheat oven to 350°. Process cookies in food processor into fine crumbs. Combine cookie crumbs and melted butter in a large bowl; mix well.

STEP 2 Press crumb mixture onto a 12-inch pizza pan. Bake for 10 minutes. Remove from oven, and cool completely.

STEP 3 Spread softened ice cream over cookie crust. Sprinkle with Junior Mints, and drizzle with melted chocolate. Freeze 1 hour or until firm.

Shopping List

1 package mint Oreo® cookies (30 cookies)

4 tablespoons butter, melted

1 (1½-quart) container chocolate mint chip ice cream, softened

1 (4-ounce) box Junior Mints® candy

½ cup chocolate chips, melted

MarkCharles Says:

"Get everyone involved in making this yummy treat, then enjoy it served on a pizza stone for the full "PIZZA LOOK!"

notes:

Tip

No time to freeze? Soften ice cream slightly until easy to scoop. Top crust evenly with scoops of ice cream, sprinkle with candy, drizzle with chocolate and serve.

PREP	COOK	SERVES
20 min	50 min	10

Christy's College Carrot Cake

Shopping List

For Cake:

2 cups all-purpose flour

2 teaspoons cinnamon

2 teaspoons baking powder

1 teaspoon baking soda

1 teaspoon salt

1 teaspoon unsweetened cocoa

4 large eggs

1 cup sugar

1 cup dark brown sugar

1½ cups vegetable oil

2 teaspoons vanilla extract

4 cups grated carrots

1 cup chopped walnuts

For Icing:

2 (8-ounce) packages cream cheese, softened

½ cup butter, softened

2 cups confectioners' sugar

1 teaspoon vanilla extract

STEP 1 Preheat oven to 350°. Grease 2 (9-inch) cake pans, and line with parchment paper.

STEP 2 Combine flour, cinnamon, baking powder, baking soda, salt and cocoa in a medium bowl; set aside.

STEP 3 Beat eggs with sugars, oil and vanilla with an electric mixer on medium speed until well combined. Gradually add flour mixture, and beat on low speed, until flour mixture is just incorporated. Fold in carrots and walnuts.

STEP 4 Pour batter into prepared pans, and bake for 40 minutes or until toothpick inserted in center comes out clean. Cool in pans on wire racks for 10 minutes. Remove from pans, and cool completely on wire racks.

STEP 5 For icing, set mixer on medium speed; beat cream cheese and butter until smooth. Gradually beat in confectioners' sugar and vanilla until smooth.

STEP 6 Place 1 cake layer on cake plate. Spread with half the frosting. Top with remaining cake layer, and spread with remaining frosting.

STEP 7 Refrigerate until ready to serve.

Tip

Add 1 teaspoon grated orange zest to icing for Creamsicle® flavor.

PREP	COOK	MAKES
20 min	65 min	2 loaves

Meme's Absolutely Nuts Zucchini Bread

STEP 1 Preheat oven to 350°. Spray 2 (9x5-inch) loaf pans with cooking spray. Sprinkle pans with flour.

STEP 2 Combine flour, baking soda, cinnamon, salt and baking powder in a medium bowl, and set aside.

STEP 3 Beat eggs with sugar, oil and vanilla with an electric mixer on medium speed until well combined. Gradually add flour mixture, and beat on low speed until flour mixture is just incorporated. Fold in zucchini, walnuts and raisins.

STEP 4 Pour batter into prepared pans, and bake for 55 minutes or until wooden pick inserted in center comes out clean. Cool in pans on wire racks for 10 minutes. Remove from pans, and cool completely on wire racks.

Shopping List

3½ cups all-purpose flour
1½ teaspoons baking soda
1 teaspoon cinnamon
1 teaspoon salt
¾ teaspoon baking powder
4 large eggs
2 cups sugar
1 cup vegetable oil
1½ teaspoons vanilla extract
2 cups peeled and grated zucchini
1 cup chopped walnuts
1 cup raisins

Tip

Eat one loaf now, and freeze the second for later. Wrap tightly with plastic wrap, and freeze. When ready to use, simply thaw overnight at room temperature.

Mom Pez's Mini Cappuccino Pies

PREP	COOK	MAKES
20 min	10 min	12

Mom Pez's Mini Cappuccino Pies

STEP 1
Heat chocolate, sugar, rum, espresso powder and vanilla in a double boiler. Stir frequently until chocolate melts and mixture is smooth. Stir in egg yolks, and cook for 5 minutes, stirring frequently until mixture is hot and thickens slightly. Remove from heat, and let cool.

STEP 2
With electric mixer on medium high, beat heavy cream in a large bowl until soft peaks form.

STEP 3
Fold cooled chocolate mixture into heavy cream. Spoon into mini pie crusts.

STEP 4
Refrigerate 4 hours or until firm. Serve with additional whipped cream, if desired.

Shopping List

3 (1-ounce) squares unsweetened chocolate

½ cup sugar

3 tablespoons dark rum

2 tablespoons instant espresso powder

2 teaspoons vanilla extract

4 large egg yolks

8 ounces heavy cream

12 mini graham-cracker pie crusts

Tip

Substitute different liquors for flavor variation. Instead of rum, try tequila, Grand Marnier or Bailey's®.

PREP	COOK	SERVES
10 min	8 min	6

SUMMER

Open-Faced Waffles and Ice Cream with Strawberry Basil Sauce

Shopping List

2 cups sliced strawberries

½ cup strawberry jam

2 tablespoons chopped fresh basil

1 tablespoon lemon juice

Pinch of salt

6 waffles, toasted

3 cups vanilla ice cream

 STEP 1 Combine strawberries, jam, basil, lemon juice and salt in a small saucepan. Bring to a boil over medium-high heat. Reduce heat to low, and simmer for 5 minutes or until strawberries soften.

 STEP 2 Top each waffle with a ½ cup scoop of ice cream and ¼ cup sauce.

notes:

Tip

Experiment with different berries and herbs; try blueberries with thyme, blackberries with pineapple sage or mixed berries with mint.

PREP	COOK	MAKES
10 min	18 min	10

Island Grilled Pineapple Tart

STEP 1 Preheat oven to 450°. Line a 10-inch tart pan with pie crust. Flute edges, and trim as necessary. Pierce crust all over with a fork. Bake 8–10 minutes until golden. Remove and cool.

STEP 2 Combine melted butter with 2 tablespoons brown sugar. Grill pineapple slices for 8 minutes, brushing with brown sugar mixture, turning once, until tender and browned.

STEP 3 Combine cream cheese, remaining brown sugar and rum, and beat with an electric mixer until smooth.

STEP 4 Spread cream cheese mixture evenly over crust. Top with grilled pineapple slices, overlapping, if necessary. Sprinkle with coconut and macadamia nuts. Serve immediately, or chill, if desired.

Shopping List

1 (9-inch) refrigerated pie crust

2 tablespoons butter, melted

5 tablespoons brown sugar, divided

6 (½-inch-thick) pineapple slices

1 (8-ounce) package cream cheese, softened

2 tablespoons coconut-flavored rum

½ cup coconut, toasted

½ cup chopped macadamia nuts, toasted

notes:

Tip

If you don't have a tart pan, simply bake a free-form crust. Roll dough to a 12-inch circle. Arrange on parchment paper on baking sheet. Fold edge in about ½ inch, and crimp with fingers. Bake as above.

Grandmere Muzia's Veal Stew

PREP	COOK	SERVES
30 min	3 hours	6

Grandmere Muzia's Veal Stew

Shopping List

2 pounds veal stew meat, cut in 1½-inch cubes

Salt and freshly ground black pepper to taste

2 tablespoons flour

3 tablespoons canola oil, divided

1 large onion, chopped (2 cups)

4 medium carrots, peeled and sliced into ½-inch rounds (1½ cups)

2 tablespoons tomato paste

1 cup dry white wine

2 cups low-sodium chicken broth

1 dried bay leaf

1 teaspoon dried thyme

8 ounces frozen pearl onions, thawed (1 cup)

2 tablespoons chopped fresh parsley

STEP 1 Season veal with salt and pepper. Sprinkle with flour.

STEP 2 Heat a heavy-gauge pot over medium-high heat. Add 2 tablespoons oil. Add veal in batches, making sure not to overcrowd the pot. Sear on both sides. Set meat aside with a slotted spoon in a dish.

STEP 3 Add remaining oil to saucepot. Add onion and carrots, and cook about 5 minutes or until beginning to soften. Add tomato paste, wine, broth, bay leaf and thyme. Bring to a boil, then reduce heat to simmer. Add veal and any juices in the dish.

STEP 4 Cover saucepot, and cook for 1½–2 hours.

STEP 5 Add pearl onions, and cook for 15 minutes.

STEP 6 Garnish with parsley immediately before serving.

Tip

Serve over rice or noodles. Try adding frozen peas to the stew and the zest of 1 lemon at the end of cooking.

PREP	COOK	SERVES
10 min	1 hour	12

Brined Turkey Breast

STEP 1 Combine broth, orange juice, bay leaves, pepper-corns, salt and sugar in 1-quart glass measuring cup. Stir well.

STEP 2 Arrange turkey breast and herbs in plastic bag, and pour broth mixture over turkey. Toss to coat. Close bag, and place in a shallow baking dish. Refrigerate 12 hours or overnight.

STEP 3 Preheat oven to 425°. Remove turkey from bag; discard brine.

STEP 4 Arrange turkey breast in small shallow roasting pan. Roast 15 minutes. Pour 1 cup water over turkey. Lower oven temperature to 375°. Continue roasting, basting frequently with juices on bottom of pan, for 45 minutes or until internal temperature reaches 170°. Let stand 10 minutes. Cut away tie, and thinly slice.

notes:

Shopping List

2 cups unsalted or low-sodium chicken or vegetable broth or stock

½ cup orange juice

3 torn bay leaves

1 tablespoon whole peppercorns, crushed

⅓ cup fine sea salt

Pinch of sugar

1 tied boneless turkey breast roast (3 pounds)

1 cup water

Tip

Decorate turkey platter with quartered oranges, fresh thyme, and rosemary sprigs.

FALL

PREP	COOK	SERVES
20 min	30 min	6

Cheesy Cauliflower Bake

Shopping List

1 head cauliflower
1 cup water
2 tablespoons butter
2 tablespoons flour
¼ teaspoon dry mustard
¼ teaspoon salt
⅛ teaspoon cayenne pepper
⅛ teaspoon ground pepper
1½ cups milk
1 cup shredded Cheddar cheese
2 slices bacon
½ cup panko bread crumbs

STEP 1 Preheat oven to 350°.

STEP 2 Remove outer leaves from cauliflower. Core, and separate into florets. Place in large saucepan with 1 inch water. Bring to a boil. Reduce heat to low, cover and cook for 8–10 minutes or until tender. Drain.

STEP 3 Place cauliflower in food processor in batches, and pulse 4–5 times to coarsely chop. Do not purée. Spray a 2-quart casserole with cooking spray. Pour cauliflower into casserole.

STEP 4 Melt butter in 1-quart saucepan over medium heat. Stir in flour. Cook for 2 minutes, stirring constantly. Stir in mustard, salt and peppers. Slowly stir in milk. Bring to a boil, and stir until slightly thickened. Stir in cheese. Pour evenly over cauliflower.

STEP 5 In small skillet, cook bacon until crisp. Drain and crumble. Spoon 2 tablespoons of bacon fat into the bread crumbs. Sprinkle bacon and bread crumbs over cauliflower.

STEP 6 Bake for 30 minutes or until heated through.

Tip

If a food processor is not available, use a potato masher to prepare cauliflower.

notes:

PREP	COOK	SERVES
15 min	45 min	8

Cream of Butternut Squash Soup with Cranberry Drizzle

STEP 1 Melt butter in a large saucepot over medium heat. Add squash and onions. Cover, and cook for 15 minutes or until squash begins to soften, stirring occasionally.

STEP 2 Add broth and thyme. Reduce heat to medium-low. Cover, and cook for 30 minutes or until squash is tender.

STEP 3 Purée soup mixture in batches in a blender or processor. Return to saucepot, and stir in half-and-half. Add salt and pepper. Heat through.

STEP 4 Purée cranberry sauce in blender until very smooth. With blender running, add a few drops of water until thin enough to pour. Using a spoon, drizzle several thin lines of sauce over soup before serving.

Shopping List

¼ cup butter or margarine

4 pounds butternut squash, peeled, seeded, cut into 1-inch cubes

2 large onions, chopped (about 2 cups)

6 cups chicken broth

2 tablespoons chopped fresh thyme, or 2 teaspoons dried thyme

½ cup half-and-half

Salt and pepper to taste

½ cup jellied cranberry sauce

FALL

MarkCharles Says:

"Serving this soup in wide-mouth coffee cups or mugs creates a whole new food experience."

notes:

 Tip

For ease in making the cranberry drizzle, use a needle-nose plastic bottle (sold in craft stores). This recipe can be made a day ahead. Simply cover and refrigerate.

PREP	COOK	SERVES
10 min	25 min	4

Kielbasa with Onion, Apple and Sauerkraut

Shopping List

1 tablespoon olive oil

1 pound kielbasa, cut into 1-inch pieces

1 teaspoon caraway seed

1 large onion, chopped (about 1 cup)

1 Granny Smith apple, peeled, cored and cubed (about 1 cup)

1 (32-ounce) bag fresh sauerkraut, drained

1 cup chicken broth or stock

1 bay leaf

1 teaspoon brown sugar

½ teaspoon salt

STEP 1 Heat oil in a Dutch oven over medium-high heat. Add kielbasa, and cook until brown. Stir in caraway seed. Cook 1 minute. Stir in onion and apple. Cook for 3 minutes or until onion is tender.

STEP 2 Add the sauerkraut, broth, bay leaf, sugar and salt. Bring to a boil.

STEP 3 Cover and cook over low heat for 30 minutes or until mixture is thoroughly heated, stirring occasionally. Remove bay leaf before serving.

notes:

Tip

Serve on a platter with a ring of mashed potatoes around the outside.

PREP	COOK	SERVES
10 min	20 min	4

Parmesan and Garlic Encrusted Brussels Sprouts

STEP 1 Brown bacon in a large skillet on medium-high heat; drain bacon on paper towels. Remove all but 2 tablespoons drippings.

STEP 2 Add Brussels sprouts to skillet, and cook for 3 minutes or until slightly browned, stirring occasionally.

STEP 3 Stir in garlic, and reduce heat to low. Add broth, and bring to a boil. Cover, and cook 10 minutes or until sprouts are tender. Pour into serving dish. Toss with bacon.

STEP 4 Melt butter in a small pan, and stir in bread crumbs. Cook over medium-low heat until crumbs are golden brown. Stir in cheese. Sprinkle crumb mixture over sprouts.

Shopping List

3 slices bacon, chopped

1 pound Brussels sprouts, trimmed, larger ones halved

4 garlic cloves, peeled and thinly sliced

¼ cup chicken broth or water

1 tablespoon butter

½ cup panko bread crumbs

½ cup shredded Parmesan cheese

FALL

 Tip

This recipe can be made ahead up to the step of sprinkling with crumb mixture. Finish in 350° oven for 15 minutes; sprinkle with crumb mixture immediately before serving.

PREP	COOK	SERVES
10 min	15 min	2

Cheese Tortellini with Roasted Garlic Herb Sauce

Shopping List

1 small head garlic, ½ inch sliced off top horizontally

2 tablespoons extra virgin olive oil, divided

1 medium sweet onion, chopped

3 tablespoons all-purpose flour

¼ cup white wine

2 cups low-sodium chicken broth

2 tablespoons heavy or light cream

1 tablespoon finely chopped fresh thyme leaves

1 tablespoon finely chopped fresh sage leaves

1 tablespoon finely chopped fresh parsley

1 teaspoon salt

¼ teaspoon ground black pepper

1 (9-ounce) package refrigerated cheese tortellini, cooked according to package directions

 STEP 1 Preheat oven to 400°. Arrange garlic on piece of aluminum foil, and drizzle with 1 tablespoon oil. Loosely close foil, and roast 25 minutes. Let cool slightly, and press out roasted garlic from cloves. Smash lightly with side of chef's knife; set aside.

 STEP 2 Heat remaining 1 tablespoon oil in a 12-inch nonstick skillet over medium-high heat. Cook onion, stirring occasionally, 5 minutes or until starting to brown. Add garlic, and cook 30 seconds or until fragrant. Sprinkle with flour, and continue cooking, stirring constantly 2 minutes or until slightly toasted. Add wine, and remove any burnt bits. Whisk in chicken broth, and bring to a boil over high heat. Reduce heat, and stir in cream, herbs, salt and pepper. Simmer until thickened, stirring frequently. Add in cooked tortellini, and toss to coat.

notes:

Tip

Try substituting basil for sage for a springtime herb sauce. For a more colorful version, toss in 1 cup halved cherry or grape tomatoes with tortellini. Recipe can easily be doubled.

PREP	COOK	SERVES
35 min	15 min	4

Individual Thanksgiving Casseroles

STEP 1 Preheat oven to 400°.

STEP 2 Melt butter in medium saucepan. Add celery and onion, and cook until onion is tender, stirring occasionally. Remove from heat. Add broth and stuffing to saucepan; mix lightly.

STEP 3 Stir in gravy, cranberries, thyme and pecans.

STEP 4 Spoon mixture into 4 (1-cup) gratin dishes. Place on a baking sheet. Bake 15 minutes or until hot.

Shopping List

2 tablespoons butter

¼ cup chopped celery

¼ cup chopped onion

1 cup chicken broth

2 cups herb-seasoned stuffing

1 (10½-ounce) can turkey gravy

½ cup dried cranberries

1 tablespoon chopped fresh thyme,
  or 1 teaspoon dried thyme

¼ cup chopped pecans, toasted

MarkCharles Says:

"This recipe takes all the layers of intimidation out of Thanksgiving so you can give thanks more often."

notes:

Tip

For easy cleanup, spray dishes with cooking spray before filling. This recipe can be prepared in advance and refrigerated before baking. Remove from refrigerator 15 minutes before heating.

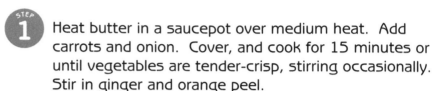

Fall

PREP	COOK	SERVES
10 min	45 min	6

Cream of Carrot Soup with Whole-Grain Croutons

Shopping List

¼ cup butter or margarine

2 pounds carrots, peeled and thinly sliced (about 5 cups)

1 large onion, chopped (about 1 cup)

1 tablespoon minced fresh ginger

1 teaspoon grated orange peel

5 cups chicken broth, divided

½ cup heavy cream or half-and-half

Salt and pepper to taste

Whole-grain croutons

STEP 1 Heat butter in a saucepot over medium heat. Add carrots and onion. Cover, and cook for 15 minutes or until vegetables are tender-crisp, stirring occasionally. Stir in ginger and orange peel.

STEP 2 Add 2 cups of broth; reduce heat to medium-low. Cover, and cook for 30 minutes or until carrots are tender.

STEP 3 Purée soup mixture in batches in a blender or processor. Return to saucepot, and stir in remaining broth, cream, salt and pepper. Heat through.

STEP 4 Top with croutons.

 Tip

Sprinkle with chopped parsley before serving. Can be made a day ahead. Simply cover and refrigerate.

FALL

PREP	COOK	SERVES
30 min	25 min	6

Turkey Skillet Pie

STEP 1
Preheat oven to 350°.

STEP 2
Melt butter in 10-inch oven-proof skillet. Add celery and onion, and cook until vegetables are tender, stirring occasionally.

STEP 3
Stir in poultry seasoning, salt and pepper. Cook for 1 minute. Stir in soup and milk, and bring to a boil. Reduce heat to low. Add turkey, and heat through.

STEP 4
Put sweet potatoes in a saucepan with enough water to cover by 1 inch. Cover, and bring to a boil. Reduce heat to low, and cook about 20 minutes or until sweet potatoes are tender. Drain sweet potatoes, and return to saucepan.

STEP 5
Using a hand mixer on low speed, beat sweet potatoes until just mashed. Add orange juice and nutmeg; raise speed to medium, and continue beating until smooth. Spread sweet potatoes evenly over turkey mixture. Bake for 25 minutes or until heated through.

Shopping List

2 tablespoons butter

1 cup thinly sliced celery

1 large onion, chopped (1 cup)

1 teaspoon poultry seasoning

½ teaspoon salt

¼ teaspoon ground pepper

1 (10¾-ounce) can cream of celery soup

½ cup milk

2 cups shredded cooked turkey

2 pounds sweet potatoes, peeled and cut into 2-inch pieces

¼ cup orange juice

⅛ teaspoon ground nutmeg

FALL

notes:

Tip

Sweet potatoes can also be mashed by hand or put through a food mill.

PREP	COOK	SERVES
10 min	25 min	4

Hearty Lasagna Soup

Shopping List

1 pound 80% lean ground beef

1 large clove garlic, minced

½ teaspoon Italian seasoning

1 (14½-ounce) can beef broth

1 (14½-ounce) can diced tomatoes, undrained

2 cups wide egg noodles

¼ cup grated Parmesan cheese

 STEP 1 Cook beef in a large saucepot. Drain off drippings. Stir in garlic and seasoning. Cook for 1 minute.

 STEP 2 Stir in broth and tomatoes. Bring to a boil. Add the noodles, and cook for 10 minutes or until noodles are tender. Stir in cheese before serving.

 **MarkCharles Says:**

"Think outside of the plate for presentation, and serve this soup in shaped pans or dishes usually used for something else—like mini loaf pans."

 Tip

Serve soup hot, topped with shredded mozzarella cheese and chopped basil.

notes:

FALL

PREP	COOK	SERVES
30 min	15 min	4

Turkey Pot Pie with Onion Biscuits

STEP 1 Preheat oven to 425°.

STEP 2 Heat oil in a 10-inch oven-proof skillet over medium heat. Add pancetta, and cook until brown and crispy, stirring occasionally. Remove from skillet, and drain.

STEP 3 Add butter, onion, carrots, salt and pepper. Cook until carrots are tender. Stir in flour, and cook for 1 minute. Stir in broth, and stir to deglaze pan. Cook until mixture thickens, about 3 minutes, stirring frequently.

STEP 4 Add pancetta, cream, turkey and peas.

STEP 5 Combine baking mix and dry onion soup mix in a medium bowl. Slowly stir in milk until moistened. If mixture seems too dry, add more milk by tablespoons until moist. Do not overmix.

STEP 6 Drop batter by heaping tablespoons over turkey mixture. Place skillet in oven, and bake for 15 minutes or until biscuits are golden brown.

Shopping List

- 2 tablespoons olive oil
- 4 ounces chopped pancetta
- 2 tablespoons butter
- 1 large onion, chopped (about 1 cup)
- 1 cup thinly sliced carrots
- ½ teaspoon salt
- ¼ teaspoon ground pepper
- ¼ cup flour
- 2½ cups chicken broth
- ¼ cup heavy cream or half-and-half
- 2 cups chopped cooked turkey
- 1 cup frozen peas, thawed
- 2 cups baking mix
- 1 (1-ounce) envelope dry onion soup mix
- ⅔ cup milk

notes:

PREP	COOK	SERVES
10 min	10 min	9

Herbed Cheese Biscuits

Shopping List

2¼ cups baking mix

⅔ cup milk

1 tablespoon chopped fresh thyme, or 1 teaspoon dried thyme

1 tablespoon chopped fresh chives, or 1 teaspoon dried chives

½ cup shredded Cheddar cheese

 STEP 1 Preheat oven to 450°.

 STEP 2 Combine baking mix, milk, thyme, chives and cheese in a medium bowl. Stir until a soft dough forms. Place dough on a floured surface, and knead 10 times. Roll dough ½ inch thick. Cut with a 2½-inch-diameter cookie cutter to make 9 biscuits. Place on ungreased cookie sheet.

 STEP 3 Bake 8–10 minutes or until golden brown.

notes:

Tip

Any fresh herb can be substituted for the thyme and chives.

FALL

Herbed Cheese Biscuits

PREP	COOK	SERVES
10 min	20 min	8

Sausage Cranberry Strudel

Shopping List

1 pound bulk pork sausage

5 tablespoons butter or margarine

1 large onion, chopped (about 1 cup)

1 cup chopped celery

2 cups chicken broth

1 (12-ounce) package cubed seasoned stuffing

½ cup dried cranberries

1 (9-inch) refrigerated pie crust

1 egg, beaten with 1 teaspoon water

STEP 1 Preheat oven to 375°.

STEP 2 In large saucepan, brown sausage, breaking apart with a fork. Remove, and set aside.

STEP 3 Add butter, onion and celery to the saucepan, and cook about 4 minutes or until onion is tender. Stir in broth, stuffing, cranberries and cooked sausage. Toss well.

STEP 4 Arrange about 3 cups stuffing mixture on each pie crust, leaving about 1 inch around edges. Roll up each jellyroll style. Pinch ends together, and turn under to seal. Place seam side down on baking sheet. Brush with egg mixture. With a sharp knife, cut 3 slits on top of each pastry.

STEP 5 Bake for 25–30 minutes or until golden brown. Let stand 5 minutes before slicing.

Tip

Freeze any leftover stuffing mixture for another use.

MarkCharles Says:

"Don't you love to change things up a bit? Stuffing is never boring as a side dish strudel!"

notes:

PREP	COOK	SERVES
10 min	20 min	8

Herbed-Seasoned Cornbread and Chorizo Stuffing

STEP 1 Heat oil in large saucepot. Add sausage, and cook over medium-high heat, breaking sausage apart with a fork. Remove, and set aside.

STEP 2 Add butter to saucepot. Cook celery, onion, red pepper, chili powder and cumin until vegetables are tender, stirring occasionally. Stir in broth. Bring to a boil. Remove from heat. Stir in stuffing, and toss until blended. Stir in cooked sausage.

Shopping List

1 tablespoon oil

1 pound chorizo sausage, casings removed

5 tablespoons butter

1 cup chopped celery

1 cup chopped onion

½ cup chopped red bell pepper

1 tablespoon chili powder

½ teaspoon ground cumin

2 cups chicken broth

1 (14-ounce) package cornbread stuffing

FALL

notes:

Tip

Stuffing can be made ahead of time and put into a 2-quart casserole. Bake for 30 minutes at 350°.

PREP	COOK	SERVES
10 min	25 min	4

Cranberry Dijon Pork Tenderloin

Shopping List

- 2 pork tenderloins (about 1¼ pounds each)
- 1 teaspoon salt
- ½ teaspoon ground pepper
- 2 tablespoons olive oil
- ¼ cup Dijon mustard
- 1 tablespoon minced shallots
- 3 garlic cloves, minced
- ¾ cup white wine
- ¼ cup heavy cream or half-and-half
- ½ cup dried cranberries

 STEP 1 Preheat oven to 375°.

 STEP 2 Sprinkle pork with salt and pepper. Heat oil in a 12-inch oven-proof skillet over medium-high heat. Cook pork until golden brown, about 3 minutes on each side. Place skillet in oven, and roast for 15–20 minutes or until internal temperature reaches 160°. Remove pork from skillet, cover and set aside.

 STEP 3 Add mustard, shallots, garlic, and wine to skillet; stir to deglaze pan. Bring to a boil. Stir in cream and cranberries.

 STEP 4 Slice pork and serve with sauce.

 Tip

If the skillet handle is not oven-proof, cover handle with aluminum foil.

FALL

PREP	COOK	SERVES
10 min	30 min	8

Savory Herb Stuffing with Granny Smith Apples

STEP 1 Preheat oven to 350°.

STEP 2 Melt butter in large saucepan. Add onion, celery, carrots and apple. Cook over medium-high heat until vegetables are tender, stirring occasionally.

STEP 3 Add broth, and bring to a boil. Remove from heat. Stir in stuffing, craisins, and nuts, and toss until blended.

STEP 4 Spoon into a 2-quart casserole. Bake covered for 30 minutes or until heated through.

notes:

Shopping List

5 tablespoons butter or margarine

1 large onion, chopped (about 1 cup)

1 cup chopped celery

1 cup shredded carrots

1 Granny Smith apple, peeled, cored and chopped (about 1 cup)

2 cups chicken broth

1 (14-ounce) package herb-seasoned stuffing

1 cup craisins

½ cup chopped walnuts, toasted

FALL

Tip

For crunchier stuffing, bake uncovered. Spray casserole with cooking spray for easy clean up.

PREP	COOK	SERVES
20 min	20 min	6

Smokey Chicken Pot Pies

Shopping List

- 4 slices thick, center-cut bacon
- 1 pound boneless, skinless chicken breasts, cut into small chunks
- 1 small sweet onion, chopped
- 1 teaspoon dried thyme leaves
- ¼ teaspoon salt
- ¼ teaspoon ground black pepper
- 2 tablespoons white wine
- 1 (10¾-ounce) can condensed cream of chicken soup
- ½ cup milk
- 1 (10-ounce) package frozen peas and carrots, thawed
- 1 (10-ounce) package frozen puff pastry shells, cooked according to package directions (6 shells)

 STEP 1 Brown bacon in 12-inch nonstick skillet until crisp. Remove from pan and coarsely chop. Reserve 2 tablespoons bacon drippings. Wipe out any browned bits with paper towel.

 STEP 2 Heat bacon drippings over medium-high heat. Add chicken and onion, stirring occasionally, and cook for 5 minutes or until chicken is browned and onion is softened. Sprinkle with thyme, salt and pepper. Add wine, and bring to a boil. Add soup and milk, and bring to a boil. Reduce heat, and simmer 3 minutes or until thickened. Stir in peas and carrots, and heat through. Crumble, and stir in half the bacon.

 STEP 3 Spoon into pastry shells. Sprinkle each with remaining bacon.

notes:

 Tip

Substitute
1 tablespoon fresh
thyme leaves for the
dried thyme.

FALL

Smokey Chicken Pot Pies

Fall

Savory Sweet Potato Turnovers

Shopping List

1 cup prepared or leftover mashed sweet potatoes

1 tablespoon brown sugar

¼ teaspoon dried thyme

¼ teaspoon ground cinnamon

¼ teaspoon ground ginger

⅛ teaspoon ground black pepper

1 (9-inch) refrigerated pie crust

1 egg, beaten with 1 teaspoon water

STEP 1 Preheat oven to 400°.

STEP 2 In a blender or food processor, blend sweet potatoes with sugar, thyme, cinnamon, ginger, and pepper.

STEP 3 Unfold pie crust, and evenly cut into quarters (4 triangles).

STEP 4 Place ¼ cup sweet potato mixture in center of each triangle, and fold over to form turnover. Seal edges using fork. Brush each with egg mixture. If desired, sprinkle each with additional cinnamon and a pinch of dried thyme.

STEP 5 Arrange on baking sheet, and cook 12 minutes or until golden brown.

Tip

To make 8 mini turnovers, cut each dough triangle in half, and fill each with 2 tablespoons of potato mixture.

FALL

PREP	COOK	SERVES
30 min	30 min	6

Creamy Mashed Potato Bake

STEP 1 Preheat oven to 350°.

STEP 2 Place potatoes in a medium saucepan, and add enough water to cover. Bring to a boil. Cover, and reduce heat to low. Cook until potatoes are tender, about 15 minutes. Drain and return to the sauce-pan.

STEP 3 Heat milk and butter in a small saucepan until just warm.

STEP 4 Using a hand mixer on low speed, beat potatoes until just mashed. Slowly add milk mixture, buttermilk, salt and pepper. Raise speed to medium and beat until fluffy. Stir in cheese.

STEP 5 Spoon into a 1½-quart casserole. Bake for 30 minutes or until hot.

Shopping List

2 pounds russet potatoes, peeled, cut into 1½-inch pieces

¼ cup milk

¼ cup butter

½ cup buttermilk

1 teaspoon salt

¼ teaspoon ground pepper

1 cup shredded Cheddar cheese

notes:

Tip

Serve as a potato bar with cooked crumbled bacon, chopped chives and French fried onions.

FALL

PREP	COOK	SERVES
10 min	50 min	12

Autumn Pumpkin Quick Bread

Shopping List

1 (14-ounce) box pumpkin quick bread and muffin mix

¾ cup whole berry cranberry sauce

½ cup chopped toasted pecans or walnuts

1 teaspoon grated orange peel

STEP 1 Preheat oven to 375°. Lightly spray 8x5-inch loaf pan with cooking spray.

STEP 2 Prepare pumpkin bread mix according to package directions, then stir in cranberry sauce, pecans and orange peel.

STEP 3 Turn into prepared loaf pan, and bake 55 minutes or until toothpick inserted in center comes out clean. Let cool on wire rack.

Tip

Substitute ½ cup chopped dried figs, cherries or cranberries for cranberry sauce.

MarkCharles Says:

"Pumpkin is my favorite color and this recipe is the beginning of the long-held romance with the taste of pumpkin, too!"

notes:

FALL

PREP	COOK	SERVES
10 min	25 min	6

Chicken with Herbed Pomegranate Blueberry Sauce

STEP 1 Sprinkle chicken with salt and pepper.

STEP 2 Heat butter and oil in a skillet over medium-high heat. Cook chicken on both sides until browned, about 10 minutes. Remove and set aside.

STEP 3 Add shallots, garlic, chives, parsley and thyme. Cook for 2 minutes, or until shallots are tender.

STEP 4 Stir in 1 cup pomegranate juice and broth. Stir together 2 teaspoons pomegranate juice and corn-starch. Stir into shallot mixture. Bring to a boil, and cook until slightly thickened, stirring occasionally. Stir in blueberries. Return chicken to skillet, and cook until heated through.

notes:

Shopping List

4 boneless, skinless chicken breasts (about 1½ pounds)

1 teaspoon salt

½ teaspoon ground pepper

1 tablespoon butter

1 tablespoon olive oil

¼ cup chopped shallots

1 clove garlic, minced

2 teaspoons each: chopped fresh chives, parsley and thyme

1 cup pomegranate juice plus 2 teaspoons, divided

½ cup chicken broth

1 teaspoon cornstarch

½ cup fresh blueberries

FALL

Uncle Joe's Apple
Tarte Tatin

PREP	COOK	STAND	SERVES
35 min	15 min	5 min	6

Uncle Joe's Apple Tarte Tatin

STEP 1 Preheat oven to 450°. Spray an 8-inch cake pan with nonstick spray. Place a round of parchment paper in the bottom. Spray with nonstick spray.

STEP 2 Quarter, core and peel apples. Cut the quarters into 2 or 3 pieces lengthwise, depending on the size of the apples. Place in a bowl and toss with lemon juice.

STEP 3 Set a heavy skillet on medium-high heat; melt butter, and add apples. Add sugar and toss with apple mixture. Cook until sugar is becoming golden brown and apples are tender, about 15 minutes.

STEP 4 Arrange a layer of sliced apples on the bottom of cake pan. Spoon remaining apples on top along with any caramelized sugar in the skillet. Unroll pie crust. Place pie crust on apples, tucking in the edges. Cut four vent holes around the dough.

STEP 5 Bake for 15 minutes in preheated oven. Pastry should be golden brown. Remove from oven, and let stand for 5 minutes.

STEP 6 Place a round platter on top of cake pan. Hold platter and invert. Tart will come out. Serve warm.

Shopping List

5 medium Golden Delicious apples

2 tablespoons freshly squeezed lemon juice

6 tablespoons butter

1 cup sugar

1 (9-inch) refrigerated pie crust

FALL

PREP	CHILL	SERVES
20 min	2 hours	6

Amaretto Cheesecakes in Pastry

Shopping List

1 (10-ounce) package frozen puff pastry shells

1 (8-ounce) package cream cheese, softened

¼ cup butter

⅓ cup confectioners' sugar

1 tablespoon amaretto liqueur

1 teaspoon vanilla extract

½ teaspoon orange zest

Sliced strawberries for garnish

STEP 1 Bake pastry shells according to package directions. Remove tops. Let cool.

STEP 2 Beat cheese and butter until creamy. Add sugar, liqueur, vanilla and orange zest, and beat until light and fluffy.

STEP 3 Evenly fill shells with cheesecake mixture. Garnish with sliced strawberries. Chill for 2 hours or until set.

notes:

FALL

Tip

Try other liqueurs for new flavors of cheesecake—Kahlùa®, Irish Cream® or Cointreau® for starters.

PREP	COOK	MAKES
20 min	35 min	24

Maddy's Pumpkin Cupcakes with Cream Cheese Frosting

STEP 1 Preheat oven to 375°. Spray 24 muffin cups with cooking spray, or line with paper muffin liners.

STEP 2 Combine flour, baking powder, cinnamon, nutmeg, ginger, cloves, allspice, salt and baking soda in a medium bowl, and set aside.

STEP 3 Beat butter and sugars with an electric mixer on medium speed in a large bowl until combined. Beat in eggs, one at a time. Stir in milk and pumpkin purée. Gradually add flour mixture, and mix just until incorporated.

STEP 4 Pour batter into prepared muffin cups. Bake for 25 minutes or until golden and tops spring back when lightly pressed. Cool in pans on wire racks for 10 minutes. Remove from pans and cool completely on wire racks.

STEP 5 To make frosting, beat cream cheese and butter with an electric mixer on medium speed until smooth. Gradually add confectioners' sugar, vanilla and cinnamon, and beat until light and fluffy. Frost cupcakes.

Shopping List

For Cupcakes:
2¼ cups all-purpose flour

1 tablespoon baking powder

1 teaspoon cinnamon

½ teaspoon ground nutmeg

½ teaspoon ground ginger

½ teaspoon ground cloves

½ teaspoon ground allspice

½ teaspoon salt

½ teaspoon baking soda

½ cup butter, softened

1 cup sugar

⅓ cup brown sugar

2 large eggs

¾ cup milk

1 cup pumpkin purée

For Cinnamon Cream Cheese Frosting:
1 (8-ounce) package cream cheese, softened

¼ cup butter, softened

3 cups confectioners' sugar

1 teaspoon vanilla extract

1 teaspoon ground cinnamon

FALL

PREP	COOK	SERVES
15 min	12 min	8

Cinnamon Almond Croissant

Shopping List

2 tablespoons brown sugar

½ teaspoon ground cinnamon

1 (8-ounce) package refrigerated crescent dinner rolls

3½ ounces almond paste (½ tube)

1 egg, beaten with 1 teaspoon water (optional)

STEP 1 Mix sugar and cinnamon in small bowl.

STEP 2 Unroll dinner roll dough; separate into 8 triangles.

STEP 3 Lightly roll or press almond paste into 4x4-inch square on wax paper, and cut into 8 equal pieces.

STEP 4 Place 1 piece almond paste on each triangle towards the wide end. Sprinkle each evenly with sugar mixture and roll up as directed on the package. Then tuck each pointed end underneath roll to create a more croissant look. Brush, if desired, with egg mixture.

STEP 5 Place on ungreased baking sheet, and bake at 375° for 12–13 minutes or until golden brown.

notes:

For an elegant presentation, microwave ¼ cup canned whipped white frosting in a microwave-safe, glass measuring cup for 20 seconds or until melted. Drizzle on croissants. (Icing will harden.)

FALL

Cinnamon Almond Croissant

PREP	COOK	SERVES
10 min	20 min	4

Pumpkin Pear Soup

Shopping List

¼ cup butter or margarine

1 medium onion, chopped (about ½ cup)

1 (16-ounce) can pumpkin

1 (16-ounce) can pear halves, drained and diced

3 cups milk

1 cup chicken broth

1 teaspoon salt

½ teaspoon ground cinnamon

⅛ teaspoon ground nutmeg

⅛ teaspoon ground pepper

STEP 1 Melt butter in a medium saucepan. Add onion, and cook for 2 minutes or until tender. Stir in pumpkin, pears, milk, broth, salt, cinnamon, nutmeg and pepper.

STEP 2 Bring mixture to a boil. Reduce to low heat, and cook for about 10 minutes.

STEP 3 Soup can be served as is or puréed.

MarkCharles Says:

"Serve this heavenly soup in small, baby pumpkins (hollowed-out) nestled in a martini or margarita glass. Wow!"

Tip

Frizzle a few fresh sage leaves in hot olive oil for a couple of seconds, and crumble on top of each serving.

notes:

PREP	COOK	SERVES
15 min	10 min	8

Pear and Honey Tart

STEP 1 Preheat oven to 425°.

STEP 2 Press crust into and up sides of (7x11-inch) rectangular or (8-inch) round tart pan. Pierce bottom with fork. Bake 8 minutes or until just starting to brown.

STEP 3 Blend cream cheese with 2 tablespoons honey and cinnamon in small bowl.

STEP 4 Spread cream cheese mixture onto warm crust. Arrange pears on cream cheese mixture. Combine melted butter with nutmeg, and brush onto pears.

STEP 5 Reduce oven temperature to 400°. Bake 8 minutes, or until pears are softened and crust is dark golden brown. Drizzle top with remaining 2 tablespoons honey.

notes:

Shopping List

1 (9-inch) refrigerated pie crust

½ cup cream cheese, softened

4 tablespoons honey, divided

¼ teaspoon ground cinnamon

2 ripe pears, peeled, cored and thinly sliced

1 tablespoon melted butter

Pinch of nutmeg

Tip

Garnish with sprigs of rosemary and thyme. For a gourmet twist, look for flavored honey.

FALL

PREP	COOK	SERVES
15 min	40 min	12

Pumpkin Puff Pastry Pie

Shopping List

1 (17.3-ounce) package frozen puff pastry sheets (2 sheets), thawed according to package directions

¾ cup firmly packed brown sugar

1 (15-ounce) can pumpkin

1 teaspoon pumpkin pie spice

½ teaspoon salt

3 eggs

2 teaspoons pure vanilla extract

1 (12-ounce) can evaporated milk

STEP 1 Preheat oven to 400°. Lightly spray 12-cup muffin pan with cooking spray, and set aside.

STEP 2 Roll pastry on a lightly floured surface. Using a 3½-inch diameter biscuit or cookie cutter, cut out circles of pastry, and press into bottoms of prepared muffin pan. Press pastry up the sides of cups.

STEP 3 Mix sugar, pumpkin, spice and salt in small bowl.

STEP 4 Beat eggs and vanilla in large bowl. Stir in pumpkin mixture and milk.

STEP 5 Evenly pour into prepared muffin pan.

STEP 6 Bake for 30 minutes. Reduce oven temperature to 350°, and cook for 15 minutes or until knife inserted in center comes out clean and pastry is cooked.

STEP 7 Cool completely on wire rack.

STEP 8 Serve with whipped cream and dust with pumpkin pie spice, if desired.

Tip

No cookie or biscuit cutter? Use the drinking end of a round glass. For a more elegant presentation, cut any leftover puff pastry, trimming into leaf shapes. Bake separately until golden brown, and decorate tops of pies.

notes:

PREP	COOK	SERVES
15 min	55 min	12

Sour Cream Apple Pie

STEP 1
Preheat oven to 375°.

STEP 2
Blend brown sugar, butter, flour, cinnamon and nutmeg in medium bowl until large crumbs form and set aside.

STEP 3
Mix apple pie filling, sour cream, vanilla and raisins in large bowl until well mixed.

STEP 4
Arrange pie crust on baking sheet. Pour apple mixture into pie crust, and top with crumb mixture.

STEP 5
Bake 55–60 minutes or until pie filling is bubbling and crumb mixture is golden brown. Cool completely on wire rack before serving.

Shopping List

5 tablespoons brown sugar

4 tablespoons butter, softened

4 tablespoons all-purpose flour

1 teaspoon ground cinnamon

Pinch of ground nutmeg

2 (21-ounce) cans apple pie filling and topping

1 cup sour cream

1 teaspoon pure vanilla extract

½ cup raisins

1 (9-inch) deep-dish frozen pie crust

FALL

Tip

Serve with sweetened whipped cream dusted with ground cinnamon.

notes:

MC and the twins, Sonia and Tania

Gingerbread French Toast

Winter

PREP	COOK	SERVES
12 min	8 min	4

Gingerbread French Toast

Shopping List

6 eggs

1 tablespoon molasses

1 teaspoon ground ginger

1 teaspoon ground cinnamon

¼ teaspoon ground cloves

½ teaspoon vanilla extract

3 tablespoons unsalted butter, room temperature, divided

½ (16-ounce) loaf brioche bread, cut into 8 (½-inch) slices

5 tablespoons apricot syrup

2 teaspoons confectioners' sugar

STEP 1 Combine eggs, molasses, spices and vanilla in a large, shallow bowl until well mixed.

STEP 2 Heat 12-inch nonstick pan or griddle over medium heat. Melt ½ tablespoon butter, and coat pan. Dip bread into the egg mixture, coating both sides well. Immediately place on pan or griddle, cooking 4 at a time. Cook 2 minutes each side or until golden brown and toasted. Repeat for second batch.

STEP 3 Divide toast among 4 plates. Spread remaining butter on toast, and drizzle syrup over top. Dust with confectioners' sugar.

MarkCharles Says:

"For holiday fun, use your gingerbread boy and girl cookie cutters to make pancake versions of gingerbread cookies!"

Tip

Substitute challah for brioche.

notes:

WINTER

PREP
10 min

COOK
20 min

SERVES
4

Beef Stroganoff

STEP 1
Bring salted water to a boil in a 4-quart pot over high heat. Add noodles, and cook 5–6 minutes or until tender. Drain, and reserve.

STEP 2
Whisk cornstarch and water in a small bowl. Set aside.

STEP 3
Heat oil in a 3-quart sauté pan over medium-high heat. When oil is hot, add steak. Season with salt and pepper, and sauté about 3 minutes or until browned. Remove to plate. Reserve pan.

STEP 4
Add garlic and thyme to reserved pan, reduce heat to medium, and sauté 30 seconds, or until garlic is fragrant. Add wine and reduce by two-thirds, 1–2 minutes. Stir in beef stock and pearl onions. Season with salt and pepper. Cook about 5 minutes or until onions are thawed.

STEP 5
Re-whisk cornstarch mixture, and pour into wine mixture. Cook about 1 minute or until thickened. Stir in heavy cream, and cook 1 minute, or until warm through.

STEP 6
Divide noodles among 4 pasta bowls, and top with stroganoff. Garnish with parsley.

notes:

Shopping List

½ (12-ounce) package extra wide egg noodles (about 4 cups)

2 teaspoons cornstarch

2 teaspoons cold water

2 tablespoons canola oil

1 pound filet mignon steak, about 1½-inch cubed, patted dry

Salt and ground black pepper to taste

3 garlic cloves, minced

1 tablespoon thyme leaves

½ cup Cabernet Sauvignon

1 cup beef stock

2 cups frozen pearl onions

¼ cup heavy cream

¼ cup chopped parsley

Tip

When available, buy the tail ends of the filet to save on cost.

WINTER

PREP	COOK	SERVES
10 min	40 min	5

Black Bean Soup with Ham Hocks and Sour Cream

Shopping List

3 tablespoons canola oil

1 onion, diced (1 cup)

1 teaspoon cayenne pepper

2 garlic cloves, minced

4 cups chicken stock

2 ham hocks (about 1 pound)

3 (15-ounce) cans black beans, drained and rinsed

Salt and ground pepper to taste

½ cup sour cream

1 lime, cut into wedges

STEP 1 Heat oil in a 4-quart pot over medium heat. When oil is hot, add onion and cayenne. Sauté 3–5 minutes or until tender. Stir in garlic, and sauté 30 seconds or until fragrant.

STEP 2 Add stock, ham hocks and beans. Season lightly with salt and pepper. Bring to a boil over high heat; reduce to medium-low heat, and continue cooking about 30 minutes, until flavors combine.

STEP 3 Remove and discard ham hocks. Reserve 3 cups soup. Pour remaining soup into blender with tight-fitted lid. Hold lid while puréeing until smooth. Return to pot. Stir in reserved soup.

STEP 4 Divide among 5 bowls. Top with sour cream, and serve lime on side.

notes:

Tip

For a heartier soup, add ½ cup rice during the last 15 minutes of cooking time. Cover, and simmer; do not purée.

PREP	COOK	SERVES
8 min	20 min	5

Blue Cheese Potato Soup with Olive Tapenade

STEP 1 Heat oil in 4-quart pot over medium heat. Add onion and sauté 2 minutes or until tender. Add garlic and sauté 1 minute, or until fragrant.

STEP 2 Stir in potatoes and stock. Season with salt and pepper. Bring to a boil over high heat, and cook 8–10 minutes, or until potatoes are tender. Remove from heat.

STEP 3 Stir in blue cheese until creamy. Season with salt and pepper.

STEP 4 Divide among 5 bowls, and top with tapenade and chives.

Shopping List

2 tablespoons canola oil

1 onion, diced (1 cup)

2 garlic cloves, minced

2 Idaho potatoes (about 1 pound), peeled and cut into 1-inch cubes

4 cups chicken stock

Salt and ground black pepper to taste

5 cups crumbled blue cheese

5 teaspoons prepared olive tapenade

5 teaspoons sliced chives

notes:

Tip

When dicing the potatoes, place them in a large pourable pitcher, and fill with chicken stock. This will prevent them from turning brown.

WINTER

PREP	COOK	MAKES
20 min	20 min	30

Grandmere's Meatballs

Shopping List

- 2 pounds meatloaf mix
- ½ cup grated fresh Parmesan cheese
- 1 tablespoon finely chopped fresh sage
- ¼ cup finely chopped fresh basil
- 4 garlic cloves, minced
- 1 egg, beaten
- 1 (14½-ounce) can petite diced tomatoes, drained and re-chopped
- ½ teaspoon salt
- ¼ teaspoon ground black pepper
- 1 cup fresh bread crumbs

 STEP 1 Combine meatloaf mix, cheese, sage, basil, garlic, egg, tomatoes, salt, pepper and bread crumbs in a large bowl, mixing well. Shape the mixture into 1-ounce meatballs.

 STEP 2 Bake at 400° for 20 minutes or until cooked through.

notes:

WINTER

Grandmere's Meatballs

PREP	COOK	SERVES
8 min	1 hour	8

Persian Split Pea Soup

Shopping List

1 onion, chopped (1 cup)

½ cup chopped baby carrots

2 stalks celery, chopped (½ cup)

½ teaspoon ground cumin

½ teaspoon ground cinnamon

½ teaspoon ground cardamom

⅛ teaspoon ground cloves

1 pound dried green split peas, sorted and rinsed

8 cups vegetable stock

Salt and ground black pepper to taste

STEP 1 Combine onion, carrots, celery, spices, peas and stock in a 6-quart pot. Bring to a boil. Reduce heat, cover and simmer for about 1 hour or until peas are tender. Season with salt and pepper.

STEP 2 Divide among 8 bowls.

notes:

Tip

For a thicker consistency, use 6 cups vegetable stock.

WINTER

Winter

White Bean Soup with Fennel and Sun-Dried Tomatoes

 STEP 1 Cook bacon in a 4-quart saucepan or soup pot until barely crisp. Add fennel and garlic, and cook for 5–6 minutes, or until fennel is soft. Deglaze the pan with the wine.

 STEP 2 Add beans, tomatoes, and broth, and bring to a boil. Simmer for 15 minutes. Season with basil, salt and pepper. Serve with Parmesan cheese and crusty bread, if desired.

Shopping List

- ¼ pound diced bacon
- 1 fennel bulb, diced (about 2 cups)
- 2 garlic cloves, minced
- ½ cup white wine
- 1 (15-ounce) can cannellini beans, drained
- ½ cup chopped sun-dried tomatoes
- 4 cups low-sodium chicken broth
- 3 tablespoons chopped basil or parsley
- Salt and ground black pepper to taste
- Parmesan cheese (optional)

MarkCharles Says:

"Hollow out 6 whole-grain rolls (about 5 inches in diameter) to make bread bowls. Fill with soup; use the extra bread for dipping."

notes:

WINTER

Winter

Mini Beef Wellingtons with Gorgonzola

Shopping List

4 (6-ounce) filet steaks, 1 inch thick, pat dry

Salt and ground black pepper to taste

2½ tablespoons canola oil, divided

4 shallots, sliced (about ½ cup)

2 tablespoons pinot grigio wine

1 (1-ounce) packet au jus gravy mix

All-purpose flour

1 (17.3-ounce) package puff pastry sheets (2 sheets), thawed

6 ounces Gorgonzola cheese, cut into 4 cubes

1 egg, beaten with 1 teaspoon water

Tip

To prevent the pastry breaking or becoming soggy, drain shallots carefully, and pat filets dry before and after cooking.

STEP 1 Season steaks well with salt and ground pepper on both sides.

STEP 2 Heat 2 tablespoons oil in a 10-inch skillet over medium-high heat. When oil is hot, add steaks, and sear 2 minutes on each side or until browned. Remove to paper-towel-lined plate. Set aside.

STEP 3 Add remaining oil to skillet; add shallots, and reduce heat to medium-low. Sauté 5–6 minutes or until tender. Add wine, and reduce 1–2 minutes or until dry. Remove shallots to a fine-mesh strainer, discarding excess liquid. Set aside.

STEP 4 Preheat oven to 425°. Prepare au jus according to package directions.

STEP 5 Unfold pastry, and lightly dust work surface with flour. Roll out pastry slightly to thin it, and cut into 4 squares. Divide and place shallots in the center of each square. Add cheese cubes onto shallots, and place each steak on top of the cheese (pressing down lightly).

STEP 6 Prepare second pastry sheet as in Step 5. Place squares on top of steaks, and brush the edges with egg mixture, pulling up all the sides to form a package. Brush the bottom with egg mixture, flip over and place on a parchment-lined baking sheet. Brush remaining pastry surface with egg mixture. Bake 22–23 minutes for medium doneness, or until golden brown. Remove and set aside for 8 minutes. Spoon desired amount of au jus among 4 plates, and center beef Wellington.

Winter

PREP	COOK	SERVES
30 min	45 min	4

Pork and Sauerkraut

STEP 1
Place oil in a large sauté pan over medium-high heat. Dry pork chops, and season with salt and pepper. Add to hot pan. Cook for 5 minutes each side or until nicely browned. Remove from pan.

STEP 2
Add onion, and sauté for 2 minutes or until tender. Add broth, apple butter, sauerkraut and reserved ½ cup juice. Stir to combine.

STEP 3
Return pork chops and any meat juices to pan, and bring mixture to a boil. Lower heat to a simmer, and cover with a lid. Cook for 20 minutes. Remove lid and check pork chops for doneness. When pork is cooked through, transfer to a platter.

STEP 4
Raise heat to medium-high, and cook sauerkraut mixture without lid for 10 minutes. Stir in parsley, and return pork chops to pan. Serve hot.

Shopping List

2 tablespoons olive oil

4 bone-in pork loin chops, (about 3½ pounds)

Salt and freshly ground black pepper to taste

1 large onion, halved lengthwise, cut into thin lengthwise slices (2 cups)

2 cups low-sodium chicken broth

⅓ cup apple butter

1 (32-ounce) bag sauerkraut, drained; reserve ½ cup juice

2 tablespoons chopped fresh parsley

Tip

Add 2 teaspoons of caraway seeds to sauerkraut mixture in Step 3.

WINTER

Leo, MC and Marli

PREP	COOK	SERVES
10 min	20 min	4

Margaret Mary's (Mimi's) Bean Soup

Shopping List

3 tablespoons olive oil

1 medium onion, chopped (1 cup)

1 small carrot, peeled, chopped (¼ cup)

½ celery stalk, chopped (¼ cup)

2 garlic cloves, sliced (1 tablespoon)

4 (15½-ounce) cans cannellini beans, drained and rinsed (6 cups)

2 quarts low-sodium chicken broth

1 teaspoon dried oregano

1 (8-ounce) ham steak, cut in half

1½ pounds boiling potatoes, peeled, cut into ¾-inch cubes (3½ cups)

Salt and freshly ground black pepper to taste

STEP 1 Place oil in a large soup pot, and set over medium-high heat. Add onion, carrot, and celery. Cook for 5 minutes or until tender-crisp. Add garlic, and cook for 2 minutes or until fragrant. Add beans, broth, oregano, ham and potatoes. Season with salt and pepper.

STEP 2 Raise heat to high, and bring to a boil, 5–8 minutes. Adjust heat, and simmer for 1 hour.

STEP 3 Remove ham slices, and serve hot.

Tip

Add a bay leaf. Try shredding the ham and adding it to the soup.

WINTER

PREP	COOK	SERVES
35 min	55 min	6

Uncle Joe's Lentils with Sausage

STEP 1 Place oil in a large sauté pan over medium-high heat. Add Italian sausage and chorizo, and cook for 5 minutes or until beginning to brown all over, stirring occasionally.

STEP 2 Add onion and garlic, and sauté for 5 minutes or until softened and starting to brown. Add potatoes, tomatoes, lentils, broth and herbes de Provence. Season with salt and pepper. Bring to a boil, then lower to a simmer.

STEP 3 Place a cover on the pan, and cook for 45 minutes, stirring occasionally.

Shopping List

2 tablespoons extra virgin olive oil

12 ounces sweet Italian sausage, cut into 1½-inch pieces

2 links chorizo, cut into ¼-inch rounds

1 medium onion, chopped (about ¾ cup)

4 large garlic cloves, minced (2 tablespoons)

1 pound red potatoes, peeled and chopped into ¾-inch cubes (about 2½ cups)

1 (14½-ounce) can diced tomatoes

1 (16-ounce) package lentils, rinsed

5 cups low-sodium chicken broth

1 tablespoon dried herbes de Provence

Salt and freshly ground black pepper to taste

Mimi and MC

WINTER

Tip

Try adding a bay leaf to the mixture. Also add chopped parsley before serving to brighten the dish.

PREP	COOK	SERVES
10 min	7 hours	6

Slow Cooker Chipotle Chili

Shopping List

1 pound ground beef

1 (1¼-ounce) packet chili seasoning mix

1 onion, diced (1 cup)

1 green bell pepper, diced (1 cup)

¼ cup diced chipotle peppers in adobo sauce (about 2 canned peppers)

1 (14½-ounce) can diced tomatoes

1 (15-ounce) can kidney beans, drained and rinsed

2 cups beef stock

¾ cup shredded Cheddar cheese

3 tablespoons sliced green onions

STEP 1 In a 10-inch skillet over medium-high heat, brown the beef. Drain, and place into a slow cooker.

STEP 2 Stir in seasoning, onion, peppers, tomatoes, beans, and stock until well combined. Cover, and cook on LOW for 7–8 hours.

STEP 3 Divide among 6 bowls, and top with cheese and green onions.

MarkCharles Says:

"Put blue corn chips in a zip-top bag, seal and crumble. Serve Chili in a margarita glass, topped with the chips."

notes:

Tip

If you like it spicier, add more chipotle peppers. To cool the heat, dollop sour cream on top of your chili.

WINTER

PREP	COOK	SERVES
5 min	7 hours	8

Slow Cooker Chicken and Herbs with Dumplings

STEP 1 Season chicken with salt and pepper. Place in slow cooker. Stir in onion, carrots, thyme, sage, and stock.

STEP 2 Cover, and cook on LOW for 7–8 hours or until chicken is cooked through. Remove bones; discard. Shred chicken, and return to stock.

STEP 3 Bring salted water in a 6-quart pot to a boil over high heat. Add gnocchi, and cook according to package directions. Drain well. Stir into cooker.

STEP 4 Place cornstarch in a small bowl, and whisk with 3 tablespoons cold water. Stir cornstarch mixture into stock to thicken slightly. Divide among 8 bowls. Garnish with chives.

Shopping List

1½ pounds chicken thighs, skin removed

Salt and ground black pepper to taste

1 onion, diced (1 cup)

1 cup sliced baby carrots

1½ teaspoons dried thyme

1½ teaspoons dried sage

4 cups chicken stock

1 (17.6-ounce) package potato gnocchi

3 tablespoons cornstarch

3 tablespoons cold water

¼ cup sliced chives

Tip

If you prefer, cook the gnocchi the day before, drain and refrigerate. Spread them out on a parchment paper-lined plate so they don't stick together. Before serving, stir them into the chicken stock to warm through. The stock must be hot for the cornstarch to thicken.

notes:

WINTER

PREP	COOK	SERVES
5 min	25 min	4

Cranberry Orange Wild Rice

Shopping List

1 (6-ounce) package long-grain and wild rice

⅓ cup dried cranberries

¼ cup slivered almonds

1 (11-ounce) can Mandarin oranges, drained

2 tablespoons sliced chives

STEP 1 Prepare rice according to package directions.

STEP 2 Stir in cranberries and almonds. Remove to medium serving bowl. Gently fold in oranges, and sprinkle with chives. Serve family style.

notes:

MarkCharles and Tania

WINTER

Winter

Honey and Walnut Baked Brie

 STEP 1 Preheat oven to 400°.

 STEP 2 Stir cranberries, walnuts, honey and rosemary in a small bowl.

 STEP 3 Unfold the pastry sheet on a lightly floured surface. Roll the pastry into a 14-inch square. Cut off the corners to make a circle. Spoon the cranberry mixture into the center. Top with cheese. Brush the edge of the circle with egg mixture. Fold the pastry over the cheese to cover. Trim excess pastry, and press to seal. Brush the seam with egg mixture. Place seam side down on a baking sheet. Decorate the top with pastry scraps and additional rosemary, if desired. Brush with egg mixture.

 STEP 4 Bake for 25 minutes or until pastry is golden brown. Let stand for 45 minutes.

Shopping List

⅓ cup dried cranberries

¼ cup chopped walnuts, toasted

¼ cup honey

½ teaspoon chopped fresh rosemary, or ¼ teaspoon dried rosemary

½ (17.3-ounce) package frozen puff pastry (1 sheet), thawed

1 (15-ounce) round Brie cheese

1 egg, beaten with 1 tablespoon water

notes:

Tip

Serve on a platter surrounded with red and green grapes, sliced apples and crackers.

WINTER

PREP	COOK	SERVES
30 min	30 min	4

Magoo's Herb-Roasted Chicken Wings

Shopping List

3½ pounds chicken drummettes

Salt and freshly ground black pepper to taste

¼ cup chopped garlic

2 tablespoons chopped fresh rosemary

2 teaspoons chopped fresh thyme

½ cup Dijon mustard

1 tablespoon fresh lemon zest

½ cup fresh lemon juice

3 tablespoons chopped fresh parsley

STEP 1 Preheat oven to 400°. Season chicken with salt and pepper. Place chicken in oven on 2 broiler pans. Bake for 20 minutes, turning over halfway through.

STEP 2 Combine garlic, rosemary, thyme, mustard, lemon zest and juice in a bowl. Season with salt and pepper.

STEP 3 Heat an indoor grill pan or outdoor grill to medium-high heat. Place chicken on grill, and cook until lightly charred. Brush with garlic mixture, and grill for 2 minutes on both sides or until cooked through. Sprinkle with chopped parsley, and serve hot.

notes:

Tip

The chicken can be cooked in advance, then grilled and sauced right before serving.

Magoo's Herb-Roasted
Chicken Wings

Winter

PREP	COOK	SERVES
10 min	20 min	4

Stuffed Tilapia Florentine

Shopping List

1 cup cooked rice

½ cup chopped fresh spinach leaves

⅓ cup garlic-flavored spreadable cheese

Salt and freshly ground black pepper to taste

1 pound tilapia fish fillets (about 4)

2 tablespoons butter, melted

Fresh salsa

STEP 1 Combine rice, spinach and cheese in bowl. Season with salt and pepper.

STEP 2 Evenly spread rice mixture onto fish. Roll up, and secure with toothpicks.

STEP 3 Place in baking pan, and drizzle with butter. Bake at 350° for 20 minutes or until fish flakes with fork.

STEP 4 Top with salsa, and serve.

MarkCharles Says:

"This is home-style fish faster (and better) than going out to the drive-through!"

Tip

You can substitute flounder for the tilapi in this recipe.

notes:

WINTER

PREP	COOK	SERVES
8 min	25 min	6

Quick Mac and Cheese with Mini Meatballs

STEP 1 Bake meatballs according to package directions. Remove.

STEP 2 Stir bread crumbs and garlic powder in a small bowl. Set aside.

STEP 3 Bring salted water to a boil over high heat. Cook rigatoni until al dente, according to package directions. Drain, reserving ¼ cup pasta water.

STEP 4 Reserve pot, and stir in prepared cheese product and reserved water until melted. Stir in rigatoni, Cheddar cheese, bacon and meatballs until fully coated.

STEP 5 Pour into a 2-quart casserole; sprinkle garlic bread crumbs over top. Dot with butter, and broil for 2–3 minutes or until golden. Remove to rest for 10 minutes or until set.

Shopping List

11 ounces frozen mini meatballs (about 22)

3 tablespoons Italian bread crumbs

½ teaspoon garlic powder

½ pound rigatoni (about 3 cups)

½ pound pasteurized prepared cheese product (8 ounces)

1 cup shredded Cheddar cheese

3 tablespoons bacon bits

3 tablespoons unsalted butter

notes:

Tip

For even quicker mac and cheese, eliminate the bread crumbs, garlic powder and butter, and top with crushed store-bought garlic croutons. Do not broil.

WINTER

PREP	COOK	SERVES
55 min	14 min	6

Junge Walnut Chicken Chinese Style

Shopping List

2 garlic cloves, minced (about 1½ tablespoons)

⅓ cup soy sauce

2 tablespoons cornstarch

1½ pounds boneless chicken breasts, trimmed, cut into strips ½ inch wide and ½ inch thick

½ cup chopped walnuts

3 tablespoons peanut oil or other vegetable oil, divided

2 red bell peppers, seeded, sliced into 1-inch strips (2½ cups)

1 (8-ounce) can sliced water chestnuts, drained

1 bunch green onions, trimmed, white and light green parts chopped (about 1 cup)

8 ounces snow peas (2½ cups)

1 cup low-sodium chicken broth

1 tablespoon dark sesame oil

STEP 1 Mix garlic, soy sauce, cornstarch and chicken in a large bowl. Marinate for 20 minutes. Drain chicken, and reserve marinade.

STEP 2 Heat wok or large sauté pan over medium-high heat until hot. Add walnuts to dry pan, and quickly stir for about 20 seconds or until just fragrant. Scrape nuts out of pan onto a side dish, and reserve.

STEP 3 Heat 2 tablespoons oil in hot skillet. Add peppers and water chestnuts. Stir-fry for 3 minutes. Add onions and peas, and cook for 3 minutes or until tender-crisp. Remove to a dish.

STEP 4 Add remaining oil and chicken to pan. Stir-fry chicken for about 5 minutes or until lightly browned. Return vegetables to pan along with reserved marinade and chicken broth. Stir to combine.

STEP 5 Cover with a lid, and cook for 2 minutes over medium-low heat. Stir in reserved walnuts, and drizzle with sesame oil.

Tip

Add 2 tablespoons of chopped fresh ginger to marinade. Serve with steamed rice.

Val and MC

PREP	COOK	SERVES
10 min	15 min	12

Three-Cheese Pizza Fondue

STEP 1 Combine sauce and soup in 3-quart saucepot. Bring just to a boil over medium heat. Stir in remaining ingredients, and reduce heat to low for 20 minutes or until cheeses are melted and smooth, stirring frequently.

STEP 2 Serve with dipping favorites, such as Italian bread cubes, cooked tortellini or sliced cooked sausage.

notes:

Shopping List

1 (26-ounce) jar marinara pasta sauce

1 (10¾-ounce) can Cheddar cheese soup

2 cups shredded mozzarella cheese

¼ cup shredded Parmesan cheese

1 teaspoon dried oregano

¼ teaspoon garlic powder

1 cup diced pepperoni

Tip

For a "Pizza Supreme" Fondue, stir in cooked diced green bell pepper, onion and mushrooms.

WINTER

PREP	COOK	SERVES
15 min	30 min	7

Rita's Christmas Eve Onion Soup—a French Tradition

Shopping List

2 tablespoons butter or olive oil

4 Spanish onions, peeled and diced (about 9 cups)

1 cup white wine

1 quart beef or chicken broth

2 tablespoons chopped parsley

½ teaspoon dried oregano

Salt and pepper to taste

4 thick slices Italian or French bread

4 thick slices Swiss or Gruyère cheese

 STEP 1 Melt butter or heat oil in a large saucepan or stock pot. Add onions, and cook over medium-high heat for about 15 minutes or until golden brown. Add wine, and cook for 1 minute. Add broth, parsley, oregano, salt and pepper, and bring to a boil. Reduce heat, and simmer for 20 minutes.

 STEP 2 Just before serving, place bread slices on a baking sheet. Top each with a slice of cheese, and toast in a preheated 400° oven for 5 minutes or until cheese has just melted. Ladle soup into bowls, top each serving with a cheese crouton and serve immediately.

WINTER

PREP	COOK	SERVES
15 min	45 min	4

Easy Cassoulet

STEP 1 Cook bacon in 12-inch sauté pan over medium-low heat for 10 minutes or until crisp. Remove to paper-towel-lined plate. Crumble when cooled.

STEP 2 Cook sausage in same pan over medium heat for 5–6 minutes or until brown. Remove to paper-towel-lined plate. Degrease pan, if needed, reserving about 3 tablespoons drippings in the pan.

STEP 3 Stir in onion, carrots and thyme. Sauté about 6 minutes or until carrots are tender. Add garlic and tomato paste, and sauté 1 minute or until tomato paste is caramelized. Add wine, and cook 1–2 minutes or until reduced by two-thirds. To avoid flare-ups, turn gas stove off when adding wine, and be careful when turning the flame back on.

STEP 4 Stir in broth and beans. Season with salt and pepper. Bring to a boil over high heat. Reduce heat to medium-low, and cook 15–17 minutes or until broth reduces by two-thirds. Remove from heat; fold in bacon and sausage to warm through.

STEP 5 Divide among 4 bowls, and top with crumbs.

notes:

Shopping List

6 ounces bacon

½ pound sweet sausage, sliced ½ inch thick

1 onion, diced (about 1 cup)

1 cup sliced baby carrots

1½ tablespoons thyme leaves

3 garlic cloves, minced

2 tablespoons tomato paste

½ cup Madeira wine

1 (14½-ounce) can chicken broth

2 (15-ounce) cans white beans, drained and rinsed

Salt and ground pepper to taste

½ cup crushed butter-and-garlic croutons

Tip

Place croutons in a sealable plastic bag, press out the air, zip closed and crush into crumbs, using the flat side of a meat mallet.

WINTER

PREP	COOK	SERVES
15 min	13 min	8

Easy Pastry Cream Ring

Shopping List

½ (17.3-ounce) package puff pastry sheets (1 sheet), thawed

1 egg, beaten with 1 teaspoon water

1 (11½-ounce) container whipped cream cheese

½ cup confectioners' sugar, plus extra for garnish

½ teaspoon vanilla extract

2 cups whipped topping

1 (8-ounce) can crushed pineapple, drained

STEP 1 Unfold pastry onto cookie sheet lined with parchment paper. Cut a 4-inch square in the center of the pastry. Cut square into 9 strips. Twist into your favorite shapes, and place on top of pastry. Brush with egg mixture.

STEP 2 Bake at 400° for 15 minutes or until golden.

STEP 3 Combine cream cheese, sugar, vanilla and topping in a medium bowl.

STEP 4 Cool pastry and split in half. Spread cheese mixture on bottom half of pastry. Top with pineapple. Replace top half and sprinkle with additional confectioners' sugar.

MarkCharles Says:

"For variety, change the pineapple filling to other fruit and fruit combinations, such as canned apricots, drained and sliced, or fresh strawberries and banana slices."

notes:

WINTER

Winter

PREP	COOK	SERVES
10 min	5 min	2

Mulled Red Wine and Pomegranate Juice

STEP 1 Place pomegranate juice, wine, sugar, anise, and cinnamon in a 3-quart saucepan.

STEP 2 Set on low heat for 15 minutes. Do not boil.

STEP 3 Strain spices, and discard. Serve hot in 2 large coffee cups with an orange slice in each.

Shopping List

1 (16-ounce) bottle pure pomegranate juice

½ (10-ounce) bottle dry red wine

1 tablespoon sugar

3 pods star anise

1 cinnamon stick

2 fresh orange slices

Tip

Try slices of lime in place of oranges.

WINTER

PREP	COOK	SERVES
5 min	3 min	5

Raspberry Almond Breakfast Pudding

Shopping List

¾ cup farina

5 cups 2% milk

½ teaspoon salt

6 tablespoons raspberry agave nectar

6 tablespoons light brown sugar

6 ounces raspberries, with extra for garnish

5 teaspoons sliced almonds

STEP 1 Prepare farina according to package directions, using 5 cups milk. Season with salt.

STEP 2 Remove from heat, and stir in agave, sugar and raspberries, reserving a few. Crush the raspberries against the sides of the pot using the back of a wooden spoon, saving some for garnish.

STEP 3 Divide among 5 bowls. Top with almonds, and garnish with remaining raspberries.

notes:

Tip

Substitute blueberries, blackberries or strawberries for raspberries.

Winter

PREP	COOK	SERVES
20 min	40 min	6

Napoleons with Ginger Cream and Mandarin Oranges

STEP 1 Unfold first pastry sheet on lightly floured surface. Cut into 3 strips along fold marks, then cut horizontally into 3¼-inch squares, making 9 squares. Place on baking sheet. Place parchment paper on top and place another baking sheet on top (fitted perfectly into the first baking sheet).

STEP 2 Bake at 400° for 15–20 minutes or until golden. Remove pastry sheet from baking sheets, and cool on wire racks. Repeat with second pastry sheet.

STEP 3 Combine cheese, sugar and ginger in a food processor, and purée until smooth. Use reserved orange syrup as needed to thin cheese mixture for spreadable consistency.

STEP 4 Spread 2 tablespoons cheese mixture on 1 pastry square. Top mixture with 3 orange sections, layer another pastry square, spread 2 tablespoons cheese mixture, top mixture with 2 orange sections, layer third pastry square on top and dust with confectioners' sugar. Repeat with remaining mixture, oranges and squares, making 6 Napoleons total.

notes:

Shopping List

1 (17.3-ounce) package puff pastry sheets (2 sheets), thawed

16 ounces mascarpone cheese

½ cup confectioners' sugar, plus extra for dusting

1 (4-ounce) package crystalized ginger, minced

1 (11-ounce) can Mandarin oranges, drained, syrup reserved

Tip

At a dinner party, you may want to serve with a knife and fork; these Napoleons are as messy as they are delicious.

WINTER

PREP 15 min

SERVES 6

Nanci's Punch

Shopping List

1 (7.5-milliliter) bottle champagne, chilled

1 (2-liter) bottle ginger ale, chilled

1 (10-ounce) can frozen pink daiquiri mix

1 (12-ounce) package frozen sliced strawberries

1 (12-ounce) package frozen blueberries

 STEP 1 Pour champagne, ginger ale, daiquiri mix, strawberries, and blueberries into a punch bowl, and stir. Serve cold.

WINTER

PREP	COOK	MAKES
10 min	10 min	16

Fruit and Nut Breakfast Bars

STEP 1 Line a 9-inch baking pan with foil. Spray with cooking spray.

STEP 2 Combine butter, sugar and honey in medium saucepan. Cook over medium heat for 10 minutes, or until mixture comes to a boil, stirring constantly. Boil for 1 minute.

STEP 3 Remove from heat. Stir in cinnamon, fruit, oat flakes, oats and walnuts. Press into bottom of prepared pan.

STEP 4 Cool completely. Cut into 16 pieces. Store any leftovers in an airtight container.

Shopping List

⅓ cup butter

⅓ cup sugar

¼ cup honey

½ teaspoon cinnamon

1⅓ cups mixed dried fruit, such as apricots, cranberries, apples and cherries

2 cups oat flakes cereal, crushed

1 cup quick-cooking oats

¼ cup chopped walnuts

Tip

Try substituting chocolate chips for the walnuts.

MC's Nephew Preston

WINTER

Veggie Bread Cups

Any Season

PREP	COOK	SERVES
20 min	35 min	12

Veggie Bread Cups

Shopping List

12 slices whole-wheat bread (each slice about 3½x4¾ inches)

4 large eggs, beaten well

1 cup shredded Colby-Jack or Cheddar cheese, divided

2 cups packed small fresh broccoli florets, blanched and drained (about 5 ounces)

1 large yellow squash, diced, blanched and drained (about 1½ cups)

1 large plum tomato, seeded and chopped (about 3 tablespoons)

2 tablespoons chopped fresh oregano

½ teaspoon garlic powder

⅛ teaspoon ground red pepper

STEP 1 Preheat oven to 375°. Spray 12 (3-inch) muffin pan cups with cooking spray.

STEP 2 Hold bread slice with both hands and push top and bottom crusts into "elephant ear" or "top of a heart" shape, then press firmly into muffin pan cups.

STEP 3 Bake for 10 minutes or until bread cups are lightly golden brown. Remove pan from oven. Reduce oven to 350°.

STEP 4 In medium bowl, stir together eggs, ½ cup cheese, broccoli, squash, tomato, oregano, garlic powder, and pepper. Mix well. Divide mixture evenly among muffin pan cups. Be sure to get a good mixture of veggies and egg mixture in each ¼-cup portion.

STEP 5 Bake for 25 minutes or until filling is set. Sprinkle with remaining cheese. Carefully remove each cup from muffin pan. Serve immediately.

Tip

Bread cups can be made up to 8 hours ahead. Cover, and store at room temperature. Reheat at 350° for 5 minutes before adding filling.

MarkCharles Says:

"Find your ice cream or little glass dessert dishes and mix it up with saucers from your best tea cups for a unique side dish presentation."

PREP	COOK	STAND	SERVES
15 min	50 min	10 min	6

Shortcut Ravioli Lasagna with Three Meats

STEP 1 Heat oven to 375°. Spray a 13x9x2-inch baking dish with cooking spray.

STEP 2 Combine sauce and water in a large bowl. Spread 1 cup sauce mixture in the baking dish. Top with half the ravioli, half the pepperoni, half the meat-balls, half the sausage, half the mozzarella and 1 cup sauce. Top with remaining ravioli, meats and sauce. Cover the baking dish.

STEP 3 Bake for 45 minutes or until mixture is hot and bubbly. Uncover the baking dish. Sprinkle with remaining mozzarella, and bake 5 more minutes or until melted. Let stand 10 minutes. Sprinkle with Parmesan and fresh basil. Serve immediately.

Shopping List

3 cups prepared marinara sauce

½ cup water

1 (28-ounce) package regular-size frozen cheese-filled ravioli (about 30)

½ cup halved pepperoni, slices (about 2 ounces)

8 ounces frozen, fully cooked Italian-style meatballs, 1-inch diameter (about 2 cups)

½ (1-pound) package sweet Italian sausage, cut into ¾-inch pieces (8 ounces)

1 cup shredded mozzarella cheese (about 4 ounces)

¼ cup shredded Parmesan cheese

¼ cup torn or thinly sliced fresh basil leaves

notes:

Tip

Substitute hot Italian sausage for sweet, if desired.

PREP	COOK	SERVES
25 min	20 min	6

Three-Cheese Baked Ziti with Broccoli Rabe and Hot Italian Sausage

Shopping List

- 1 (16-ounce) package uncooked medium tube-shaped pasta (ziti)
- 1 bunch fresh broccoli rabe (about 1 pound), washed, trimmed and cut into 1½-inch pieces
- 1 tablespoon olive oil
- 1 (16-ounce) package hot Italian sausage, casings removed
- 1 large onion, chopped (about 1 cup)
- 4 garlic cloves, minced
- 1 (24-ounce) jar marinara sauce
- 1 cup ricotta cheese
- 1½ cups shredded mozzarella cheese (about 6 ounces), divided
- ½ cup shredded Parmesan cheese

STEP 1 Prepare pasta according to the package directions. Add broccoli rabe during last 5 minutes of pasta cooking time. Drain well. Return to pot.

STEP 2 Heat oil for 1 minute in large skillet over medium-high heat. Add sausage, onion and garlic. Cook 5 minutes or until sausage is cooked through, breaking sausage into smaller pieces with wooden spoon, and stirring occasionally.

STEP 3 Stir sauce, ricotta and 1 cup of the mozzarella into the pasta mixture. Add sausage mixture, and stir. Spoon pasta mixture into a lightly greased, shallow 3-quart baking dish. Sprinkle with remaining mozzarella and Parmesan.

STEP 4 Bake for 20 minutes or until mixture is hot and bubbly. Serve immediately.

notes:

Tip

Substitute mild Italian sausage for the hot, if desired.

PREP	COOK	SERVES
10 min	30 min	6

Tomato Artichoke Soup

STEP 1

Heat oil in a 4-quart saucepan over medium heat. Add shallot and garlic and cook for about 3 minutes or until tender-crisp. Gradually add flour, and cook until mixture thickens, stirring constantly.

STEP 2

Gradually stir in broth. Add tomatoes and their liquid, artichokes and their liquid, lemon juice and pepper. Bring to a boil. Add basil. Reduce heat to low, and cook, covered, for 20 minutes.

STEP 3

Blend mixture using an immersion blender until smooth. Remove soup from heat. Gradually add cream, stirring well. Garnish with fresh cracked black pepper and fresh basil. Serve immediately.

Shopping List

3 tablespoons olive oil

1 large shallot, chopped (about 2½ tablespoons)

3 garlic cloves, minced

2 tablespoons all-purpose flour

5 cups low-sodium vegetable broth or vegetable stock

1 (28-ounce) can whole peeled tomatoes, undrained

1 (14-ounce) can artichokes packed in water, undrained

1 tablespoon lemon juice

¼ teaspoon ground black pepper

2 tablespoons chopped fresh basil

¾ cup heavy cream

Taylor and Mom

Tip

Substitute a regular blender or food processor for the immersion blender, but blend only ⅓ of the mixture at a time until smooth. Repeat until all the soup is blended. For a flavor twist, add 2 whole anchovies in Step 2.

ANY SEASON

PREP	COOK	SERVES
10 min	20 min	8

Spicy Chicks in a Blanket

Shopping List

½ (17.3-ounce) package puff pastry sheets (1 sheet), thawed

¾ cup honey mustard

1 (10- to 12-ounce) package fully cooked chicken sausage, any flavor (4 links)

notes:

1 Preheat oven to 400°. Unfold the pastry onto a floured cutting board. Cut off one rectangle approximately 3 inches wide, and trim to 6½ inches long. Reserve remaining square of this piece for garnish, if desired. Cut remaining pastry into 3 more rectangles along the fold lines, 3x6½ inches each. Brush approximately 1 tablespoon mustard onto each rectangle.

2 Place 1 sausage link onto each rectangle, and enclose completely in the pastry. Place seam side down onto a parchment-lined baking sheet.

3 Bake for 20–22 minutes or until golden brown. Cool slightly, then cut each link into 4 or 5 diagonal slices, and serve with remaining mustard as a dip.

Meme and Tania

ANY SEASON

PREP	COOK	SERVES
15 min	25 min	4

Steak with Tomato Gorgonzola Sauce

STEP 1 Pat steaks dry and season both sides with steak seasoning. Set aside.

STEP 2 Heat oil in a 12-inch skillet over medium-high heat. Add tomatoes, shallots and garlic. Cook, stirring often, until vegetables are tender. Add wine and stir well. Add cream and bring mixture to a boil. Reduce heat to medium, and cook until mixture thickens, about 5 minutes, stirring often. Stir in marinara sauce, cheese, rosemary and pepper. Cook, stirring often, until cheese begins to melt, about 2 minutes. Reduce heat to low, and keep warm.

STEP 3 Grill or broil steaks to medium-rare (140°) or desired doneness.

STEP 4 Plate each steak with ¼ cup sauce. Serve immediately.

Shopping List

- 4 (1-inch thick) boneless beef tenderloin steaks, 6 ounces each (filet mignon)
- 2 teaspoons Montreal steak seasoning
- 1 tablespoon extra virgin olive oil
- ½ cup plum tomatoes, seeded and diced
- ⅓ cup finely chopped shallots
- 3 garlic cloves, minced
- ¼ cup dry white wine or chicken broth
- ½ cup heavy cream
- 1 cup marinara sauce
- ½ cup crumbled Gorgonzola cheese
- 1 tablespoon chopped fresh rosemary
- ½ teaspoon freshly ground black pepper

Tip

Remove steaks from refrigerator and packaging 30 minutes to an hour before cooking. Garnish each steak's sauce portion with additional crumbled Gorgonzola cheese (about 1 teaspoon) and a sprig of fresh rosemary if desired. Serve with fresh cracked black pepper. Use remaining Tomato Gorgonzola Sauce to coat your favorite hot cooked pasta.

PREP
20 min

SERVES
4

Shaved Fennel Salad with Oranges and Black Olives

Shopping List

- 4 large navel oranges, divided
- 3 tablespoons extra virgin olive oil
- 1 tablespoon white champagne vinegar
- 1 garlic clove, minced
- 1/8 teaspoon coarse sea salt
- 1/8 teaspoon freshly ground black pepper
- 1 (5-ounce) package spring mix salad greens or baby arugula (about 4 cups)
- 2 medium fennel bulbs, trimmed, halved, cored and very thinly sliced (about 2 cups)
- 1/4 cup oil-cured black olives

 STEP 1 Trim and discard peel and pith from 3 oranges. Slice oranges crosswise into thin rounds.

 STEP 2 Juice remaining orange, and reserve 1/4 cup fresh orange juice for vinaigrette. Add juice to a small bowl and whisk in oil, vinegar, garlic, salt and pepper. Set juice mixture aside.

 STEP 3 Toss together spring greens and fennel in large bowl. Whisk juice mixture, and toss with greens mixture. Season with salt and pepper.

 STEP 4 Divide about 1 1/2 cups greens mixture onto each of 4 serving plates. Divide the orange slices and olives among the 4 salads. Serve with cracked black pepper.

 Tip

Use a mandolin or very sharp knife to slice fennel very thin for this salad.

PREP	COOK	SERVES
15 min	30 min	4

Spicy Chicken and Chorizo with Orzo

STEP 1 Heat oil in a 12-inch skillet over medium-high heat. Add onion and bell pepper, and cook until tender-crisp, stirring occasionally.

STEP 2 Stir in broth, tomatoes, orzo and red pepper. Heat to a boil, stirring frequently. Reduce heat to low. Stir in chorizo. Cook uncovered for 10 minutes or until orzo is al dente, stirring frequently.

STEP 3 Stir in chicken and cilantro. Cook for 5 more minutes or until most of the liquid is absorbed. Remove from heat and let stand, covered, for 5 minutes.

Shopping List

2 tablespoons olive oil

1 large onion, chopped (about 1 cup)

1 medium green or orange bell pepper, seeded and diced (about 1 cup)

2 cups chicken broth

1 (15-ounce) can diced tomatoes, undrained

1 cup uncooked orzo

¼ teaspoon crushed red pepper

1 (4-ounce) package chorizo sausage, coarsely chopped (about ¾ cup)

1 (10-ounce) package refrigerated fully cooked chicken breast strips (about 1¾ cups)

2 tablespoons chopped fresh cilantro

MarkCharles Says:

" Buy pita breads and toast in a skillet, about 2 minutes per side. Place them on the dinner plate as a toasty base for this meal."

notes:

For even spicier flavor, serve with hot pepper sauce.

ANY SEASON

PREP	COOK	SERVES
25 min	15 min	4

Oven-Baked Shrimp Scampi with Cavatelli

Shopping List

- 2 tablespoons olive oil
- 2 tablespoons dry white wine or chicken broth
- 1 large lemon, peeled and juiced (peel and 2 tablespoons juice reserved)
- ¼ teaspoon ground black pepper
- ¼ teaspoon coarse sea salt
- 1 pound large shrimp, peeled and deveined, with tails on
- ¼ cup fresh finely minced parsley
- 3 garlic cloves, minced
- 1 (13-ounce) package frozen cavatelli, thawed
- ½ cup butter, softened
- ⅔ cup panko bread crumbs

STEP 1
Preheat oven to 400°.

STEP 2
Combine oil, wine, 2 tablespoons lemon juice, pepper and salt in medium bowl. Add shrimp, and toss well. Let stand 10 minutes at room temperature to marinate.

STEP 3
Mince reserved lemon peel. Combine lemon peel, parsley and garlic in a small bowl. (This mixture is called gremolata). Set aside.

STEP 4
Place cavatelli evenly in 2-quart oval au gratin baking dish. Top with marinated shrimp. Pour remaining marinade over shrimp mixture. Spread butter evenly over mixture. Top mixture with gremolata, and sprinkle evenly with bread crumbs.

STEP 5
Bake for 12 minutes or until shrimp are cooked through and bread crumbs are lightly golden brown. Serve immediately.

notes:

Tip

For more browning on bread crumbs, turn oven off and heat broiler. Broil mixture 1–2 minutes or until desired brownness is reached.

PREP	COOK	SERVES
10 min	45 min	8

Mediterranean Roasted Eggplant Dip

STEP 1 Preheat oven to 400°. Cut the top off the garlic, leaving the cloves exposed. Place eggplant and garlic onto a baking sheet. Drizzle garlic with 1 tablespoon oil. Roast for 45 minutes or until eggplant is tender. Cool slightly.

STEP 2 Remove stem end of the eggplant, and squeeze garlic cloves out of the skin. Place eggplant and garlic into the bowl of a food processor. Process until smooth. Drizzle with remaining oil; season with pepper flakes, salt and pepper. Add parsley, and process once more. Cool completely, and serve at room temperature, or refrigerate until ready to use.

STEP 3 To prepare pita chips, preheat oven to 375°. Cut each pita pocket into 6–8 triangles, and separate the top from the bottom.

STEP 4 Arrange the pita triangles in a single layer on 2 large baking sheets. Brush lightly with oil, and sprinkle with salt and pepper. Toast in the oven for 8–12 minutes or until crisp. Cool completely, and store in an airtight container.

Shopping List

For Dip:

1 head garlic

1 medium eggplant, about 1½ pounds

3 tablespoons extra virgin olive oil, divided

½ teaspoon red pepper flakes

Salt and pepper to taste

½ cup packed parsley leaves

For Pita Chips:

1 (12-ounce) package pita pockets (6 loaves)

2–3 tablespoons olive oil

Salt and pepper to taste

Tip

Use prepared pita chips, if you prefer.

MarkCharles Says:

"Choose another use for your espresso cups by filling the cups with the dip and using the saucers for the chips."

PREP
10 min

COOK
25 min

SERVES
6

Loaded Baked Potato Casserole

Shopping List

6 medium russet potatoes, cut into 2-inch cubes (about 7 cups)

1 cup milk

½ cup sour cream

1 cup shredded Cheddar cheese

1 teaspoon salt

1 teaspoon ground pepper

2 tablespoons chopped chives

6 slices bacon, cooked and crumbled (about ½ cup)

1 cup French fried onions

STEP 1 Place potatoes in a 6-quart saucepot, and cover with water. Boil, and cook over medium-high heat for about 15 minutes or until tender. Drain.

STEP 2 Preheat oven to 350°.

STEP 3 Mash potatoes until smooth, and add milk, sour cream, cheese, salt and pepper. Spread potato mixture into a 3-quart baking dish, and top with chives, bacon and French fried onions.

STEP 4 Bake for 10 minutes or until onions are golden brown and crispy.

Sonia and MC

ANY SEASON

PREP	COOK	SERVES
5 min	5 min	4

Purple Haze Asparagus

Shopping List

1 pound medium asparagus, trimmed and cut into 3-inch lengths (3½ cups)

2 tablespoons extra virgin olive oil

Salt and freshly ground black pepper to taste

1 (1½-ounce) shot tequila

½ teaspoon freshly grated nutmeg

Tip

Cut asparagus on an angle.

STEP 1 Preheat large sauté pan on high heat.

STEP 2 Toss asparagus in a bowl with olive oil, salt and pepper. Add asparagus to hot pan, and stir-fry for 2–3 minutes or until tender-crisp.

STEP 3 Pour tequila into pan, and stir asparagus constantly until tequila has almost evaporated. Add nutmeg, and toss together.

STEP 4 Dish asparagus, and serve hot.

MC and Kim

PREP	COOK	SERVES
25 min	30 min	10

Potato and Broccoli Soup

STEP 1 Heat oil in a 3-quart saucepot over medium heat. Add onions and garlic and cook until tender.

STEP 2 Add potatoes, broccoli, and chicken broth, and heat to a boil. Reduce heat to low. Cover, and cook 20 minutes or until vegetables are tender.

STEP 3 Blend hot potato/broccoli mixture using an immersion blender until smooth. Stir in salt and pepper. Remove soup from heat. Serve each bowl of soup topped with Parmesan cheese and arugula.

Shopping List

2 tablespoons olive oil

1 large onion, chopped (about 1 cup)

4 garlic cloves, minced

2 pounds potatoes, peeled and diced (about 5 cups)

1½ pounds broccoli florets, coarsely chopped

5 cups chicken broth

½ teaspoon salt

¼ teaspoon ground black pepper

½ cup grated Parmesan cheese

1 cup chopped arugula

MarkCharles Says:

" Change this soup by not puréeing all of it—leave some tasty texture to savor."

notes:

Tip

Substitute a regular blender or food processor for the immersion blender but blend only ½ of the hot mixture at a time until smooth. Repeat until all soup is blended.

Any Season

PREP	COOK	SERVES
20 min	30 min	6

Grandmere's Broccoli and Cauliflower Gratin

Shopping List

1 pound broccoli, trimmed, cut into florets

1 pound cauliflower, trimmed, cut into florets

1 cup shredded Swiss cheese (about ¼ pound)

2½ cups hot milk

Pinch of nutmeg

Salt and white pepper to taste

¼ cup dry plain bread crumbs

6 tablespoons butter

STEP 1 Preheat oven to 350°.

STEP 2 Lightly grease a 1½-quart casserole dish with nonstick spray. Layer the broccoli and cauliflower in casserole dish, and top with the shredded cheese.

STEP 3 Mix the milk and seasonings together. Gradually pour the mixture over the broccoli and cauliflower.

STEP 4 Sprinkle the bread crumbs over the entire dish. Dot with butter, and bake for 30 minutes, until the liquid has been absorbed and formed a golden crust around the edges.

Tip

Add cayenne and dry mustard to cheese sauce for an extra flavor kick.

ANY SEASON

PREP	COOK	SERVES
15 min	30 min	6

Creamy Chicken Florentine

STEP 1 Heat oil in a 12-inch skillet over medium-high heat. Sauté chicken; season with salt and pepper.

STEP 2 Remove chicken from the skillet. Add half-and-half, butter and lemon juice. Whisk until thickened.

STEP 3 Add chicken to skillet, and stir. Add spinach and sun-dried tomatoes, and combine thoroughly until spinach wilts. Serve immediately.

notes:

Shopping List

2 tablespoons extra virgin olive oil

1¼ pound boneless, skinless chicken breasts, cut into 1-inch pieces

3 teaspoons salt

1 teaspoon ground black pepper

1½ cups half-and-half

2 tablespoons butter

¼ cup lemon juice

2 cups chopped fresh baby spinach

2 tablespoons chopped sun-dried tomatoes

PREP	COOK	SERVES
20 min	30 min	6

Sweet Potato Soup with Arugula

Shopping List

2 tablespoons olive oil

1 large onion, chopped (about 1 cup)

4 garlic cloves, minced

2 pounds sweet potatoes, peeled and diced (about 5 cups)

1 (32-ounce) carton chicken broth (about 4 cups)

1 cup packed, coarsely chopped baby arugula

¼ teaspoon ground black pepper

1 (4-ounce) package diced pancetta, cooked crisp and drained

6 tablespoons sour cream

STEP 1 Heat oil in 3-quart saucepot over medium heat. Add onion and garlic, and cook until tender.

STEP 2 Add potatoes and chicken broth and heat to a boil. Reduce heat to low. Cover and cook 20 minutes or until potatoes are tender.

STEP 3 Blend potato mixture using an immersion blender until smooth. Stir in arugula and pepper. Remove soup from heat. Serve each bowl of soup topped with 1 tablespoon of sour cream and ⅙ of the cooked diced pancetta.

notes:

Tip

Substitute 4 slices bacon, cooked and crumbled for the pancetta. Substitute a regular blender or food processor for the immersion blender, but blend only ⅓ of the hot mixture at a time until smooth. Repeat until all soup is blended.

PREP	COOK	SERVES
5 min	25 min	6

Italian Wedding Soup

STEP 1 Bring chicken broth, carrot and celery to a boil in a 4-quart saucepot.

STEP 2 Add orzo, reduce heat to low and simmer for 10 minutes or until pasta is al dente.

STEP 3 Mix beef, bread crumbs, egg white, oregano, salt and pepper in a medium bowl, and form into ½-inch meatballs.

STEP 4 Gently drop meatballs into the broth, and continue to simmer for about 10 minutes or until meatballs are cooked through. Add spinach, and stir until wilted.

STEP 5 Serve the soup in individual bowls. Top with cheese.

Shopping List

6 cups low-sodium chicken broth

1 carrot, finely chopped (about ½ cup)

1 stalk celery, finely chopped (about ½ cup)

1 cup orzo

½ pound ground beef

¼ cup bread crumbs

1 egg white

1 teaspoon oregano

1 teaspoon salt

½ teaspoon black pepper

1 cup chopped spinach

Shredded Parmesan cheese

MC and Dad

ANY SEASON

PREP	COOK	SERVES
15 min	25 min	4

Steak au Poivre

Shopping List

- 4 (8-ounce) boneless beef top-loin strip steaks, 1-inch thick
- 2 teaspoons coarse sea salt
- 2 tablespoons whole black peppercorns
- 2 tablespoons extra virgin olive oil
- ¼ cup unsalted butter, cut into 2 pieces
- ⅓ cup finely chopped shallots
- 2 cloves garlic, minced
- ½ cup cognac or other brandy
- ¾ cup heavy cream
- 2 teaspoons chopped fresh rosemary
- 2 teaspoons chopped fresh thyme

Tip

Remove steaks from refrigerator and packaging at least 30 minutes before cooking.

STEP 1 Pat steaks dry, and season both sides with salt. Coarsely crush peppercorns in mortar and pestle or in a sealed plastic bag with a meat pounder. Press pepper evenly on both sides of the steaks.

STEP 2 Preheat oven to 200°.

STEP 3 Heat a 12-inch heavy skillet (cast-iron preferred) over medium-high heat for 3 minutes. Add 1 tablespoon oil and cook steaks in 2 batches, turning over once, about 6 minutes per batch for medium-rare (140°). Add remaining oil to skillet before cooking second batch. Transfer steaks to an ovenproof platter and cover with aluminum foil. Keep steaks warm in oven.

STEP 4 Reduce heat to medium. Add 2 tablespoons butter to skillet. Add shallots, and garlic and cook for about 4 minutes, or until shallots are well-browned, stirring and scraping up the browned bits.

STEP 5 Add cognac with caution as it may ignite. Heat to a boil, stirring, for about 3 minutes or until liquid is reduced to a glaze. Add cream and any meat juices accumulated on platter. Bring to a boil again, stirring constantly, and cook about 5 minutes or until liquid is reduced by half. Reduce heat to low. Add remaining butter, and stir until well blended.

STEP 6 Plate each steak with 3 tablespoons shallot mixture. Top sauce with 1 teaspoon herb mixture. Serve immediately.

PREP	COOK	SERVES
10 min	25 min	6

Roasted Carrots with Sea Salt and Fresh Dill

STEP 1 Preheat oven to 400°.

STEP 2 Mix carrots with olive oil, salt and pepper in large bowl. Place carrot mixture in a single layer on shallow baking pan.

STEP 3 Roast carrots for 25 minutes or until tender-crisp, turning mixture halfway through. Sprinkle evenly with dill. Serve immediately.

notes:

Shopping List

12 fresh carrots, peeled, trimmed and cut diagonally in 1½-inch slices (about 2 pounds)

2 tablespoons extra virgin olive oil

1 teaspoon coarse sea salt

¼ teaspoon freshly ground black pepper

1 tablespoon finely chopped fresh dill

Tip

If carrots are thick, cut in half lengthwise before slicing diagonally.

PREP	COOK	SERVES
15 min	35 min	4

Easy Potato-Crusted Swiss Steak

Shopping List

1 pound sirloin

¾ cup roasted-garlic mashed potato flakes

2 tablespoons extra virgin olive oil

3 carrots, chopped (about 1 cup)

3 stalks celery, chopped (about 1 cup)

1 (14½-ounce) can crushed tomatoes, drained

1 cup beef broth

STEP 1 Cut beef into 4 (½-inch) slices.

STEP 2 Place potato flakes in a pie plate. Dredge sirloin in the flakes, turning to coat.

STEP 3 Heat oil in a 12-inch skillet over medium-high heat. Add sirloin and cook for 5 minutes or until brown on both sides. Remove steak from skillet.

STEP 4 Add carrots and celery to skillet, and cook for 3 minutes or until soft.

STEP 5 Add tomatoes and broth to skillet, and bring to a boil. Return steaks to skillet, reduce heat to low and simmer for 25 minutes.

notes:

Tania, Dad and MC

PREP	COOK	SERVES
10 min	15 min	4

Creamy Citrus Tomato Soup with Pesto Croutons

STEP 1 Preheat oven to 400°.

STEP 2 Combine soup, milk, zest and lemon juice in a 2-quart saucepan, and bring to a boil, stirring occasionally.

STEP 3 Toss bread cubes with oil and pesto in a medium bowl. Place coated cubes on a baking sheet, and cook for 5 minutes or until slightly crispy.

STEP 4 Serve soup in bowls topped with croutons.

Shopping List

2 (10¾-ounce) cans condensed orange tomato soup

2 cups milk

1 teaspoon grated lemon zest

1 teaspoon lemon juice

¼ of 1 baguette, cut into ½-inch cubes (about 1 cup)

1 teaspoon extra virgin olive oil

2 teaspoons prepared pesto

MarkCharles Says:

" Serve this delicious citrus and tomato soup in root beer mugs for a little fun"

notes:

Tip

For extra creaminess, top croutons and soup with a dollop of crème fraîche.

PREP	COOK	SERVES
40 min	30 min	8

Bacon, Leek and Herb Quiche

Shopping List

1 (9-inch) refrigerated pie crust

4 slices bacon, cooked until crisp and chopped (1 tablespoon drippings reserved)

1 tablespoon butter

2 small leeks, trimmed white and pale green parts, chopped

1 cup shredded Swiss cheese

¾ cup heavy cream

½ cup milk

3 large eggs

1 teaspoon fresh thyme

½ teaspoon salt

¼ teaspoon freshly ground pepper

⅛ teaspoon ground nutmeg

Adapted from Williams-Sonoma Comfort Food, by Rick Rodgers (Oxmoor House, 2009)

STEP 1 Heat oven to 375°.

STEP 2 Place crust on a lightly floured surface. Roll the crust into a 12-inch round.

STEP 3 Transfer to a 9-inch tart pan with a removable bottom, pressing the crust into the bottom and side of the pan. Trim the crust, leaving a ½-inch overhang. Turn excess crust under, and press it against pan, extending it about ⅛ inch above the rim. Line crust with aluminum foil, and refrigerate for 20 minutes. Fill pan with dried beans or pie weights, and place on baking sheet.

STEP 4 Bake at 375° for 20 minutes or until golden. Remove foil and beans, and cool on wire rack.

STEP 5 Heat skillet over medium heat, and add reserved drippings, butter and leeks. Cook for about 10 minutes or until leeks are tender. Remove to plate, and let cool slightly.

STEP 6 Place bacon, leeks and cheese at bottom of crust. Combine cream, milk, eggs, thyme, salt, pepper and nutmeg. Pour egg mixture into crust. Bake 30 minutes or until wooden pick inserted in middle comes out clean. Cool. Cut into wedges.

notes:

Bacon, Leek and Herb Quiche

PREP	COOK	SERVES
25 min	1 hr 35 min	8

Cheese Lasagna with Meatballs

Shopping List

2 pounds meatloaf mix

¼ cup Italian bread crumbs

2 eggs, divided

¼ cup ketchup

1 teaspoon salt

1 teaspoon oregano

1 teaspoon garlic powder

2 tablespoons parsley

2 cups ricotta cheese

2 tablespoons Parmesan cheese

1 (24-ounce) jar spaghetti sauce

8 no-boil lasagna sheets

2 cups shredded mozzarella cheese

STEP 1 Preheat oven to 375°.

STEP 2 Combine meatloaf mix, bread crumbs, 1 egg, ketchup, salt, oregano, garlic powder and parsley in a large bowl. Press meatball mixture into a 10x14-inch square on an ungreased baking sheet. Bake for 25 minutes or until cooked through.

STEP 3 Combine ricotta, Parmesan and the remaining egg in a medium bowl.

STEP 4 In a 9x13-inch baking dish, place ¾ cup spaghetti sauce. Top with 4 lasagna noodles. Spread half the cheese mixture on top of noodles. Place meatball mixture on top of ricotta, cutting in half, if necessary. Repeat layers, and top with mozzarella. Cover with foil and bake for 55 minutes or until hot and bubbly. Remove, and let stand for 15 minutes before serving.

notes:

Tip

If you prefer the look of traditional meatballs, roll the mixture into 2-inch balls and bake for 30 minutes or until cooked through. Cut them in half and place in lasagna in Step 4.

PREP	COOK	SERVES
5 min	15 min	4

Grilled Chicken Sandwich with Crushed Olive Aïoli

STEP 1 Preheat grill to medium-high. Coat chicken with oil, salt and pepper. Grill for 12 minutes or until cooked through.

STEP 2 Combine tapenade with mayonnaise and lemon juice in a small bowl.

STEP 3 Spread aïoli mixture on top and bottom cut surfaces of rolls. Add chicken, and top with cheese and arugula.

Shopping List

4 boneless, skinless chicken breasts

2 tablespoons extra virgin olive oil

1 tablespoon salt

1 teaspoon ground black pepper

¼ cup olive tapenade

2 tablespoons mayonnaise

1 tablespoon lemon juice

4 ciabatta rolls, sliced

4 slices fontina cheese

1 cup arugula

MarkCharles Says:

"Enjoy your sandwich with an arugula salad, a squeeze of lemon juice mixed with olive oil, salt and pepper."

notes:

PREP	COOK	SERVES
10 min	20 min	4

Gnocchi with Spinach and Ricotta

Shopping List

- 1 (16-ounce) package frozen potato gnocchi
- 1 (15-ounce) jar Alfredo sauce (about 1½ cups)
- ⅛ teaspoon ground nutmeg
- 2 (6-ounce) packages baby spinach
- ½ cup ricotta cheese
- ½ cup shredded mozzarella cheese

 STEP 1 Cook gnocchi according to package directions. Drain.

 STEP 2 In a 12-inch oven-proof skillet, combine sauce and nutmeg. Heat over medium heat, stirring occasionally, until mixture reduces by half. Add spinach gradually and cook about 4 minutes, or until just wilted.

 STEP 3 Remove from heat, and stir in gnocchi. Spoon ricotta in 5 large measures over gnocchi mixture. Sprinkle with mozzarella.

 STEP 4 Preheat broiler. Broil mixture 6 inches from heat for about 2 minutes or until cheese is browned and bubbling in spots.

 Tip

Delicious served with freshly cracked black pepper.

Mom

ANY SEASON

PREP	COOK	SERVES
10 min	55 min	6

Mexican Arroz con Pollo

STEP 1 Coat chicken with seasoning.

STEP 2 Heat oil in 5½-quart saucepot over medium-high heat. Sauté chicken about 7 minutes or until browned, working in batches, if necessary. Remove chicken, and add chorizo to the saucepot. Cook about 15 minutes or until cooked through. Remove and cut into ½-inch-thick slices.

STEP 3 Add onion, and cook about 5 minutes or until soft. Add tomatoes, beer, rice, chicken and sausage. Stir, and lower heat to medium low. Cover, and cook for 25 minutes or until rice is tender.

STEP 4 Stir in cilantro, and serve.

notes:

Shopping List

6 boneless, skinless chicken thighs

1 (1-ounce) envelope taco seasoning

1 tablespoon olive oil

1 pound chorizo sausage

1 small onion, chopped (about ¾ cup)

1 (28-ounce) can crushed tomatoes

1 (12-ounce) bottle lime-flavored beer

2 cups uncooked white rice

¼ cup chopped cilantro

PREP	COOK	SERVES
20 min	55 min	8

Florentine Turkey Meatloaf

Shopping List

2 pounds ground turkey

1 egg

½ cup seasoned bread crumbs

2 teaspoons salt

1 teaspoon ground black pepper

2 cups chopped fresh spinach

1 cup shredded fontina cheese

¼ cup ketchup

2 tablespoons balsamic vinegar

STEP 1
Preheat oven to 350°.

STEP 2
Combine turkey, egg, bread crumbs, salt and pepper in a medium bowl. Mix spinach thoroughly with the turkey mixture.

STEP 3
Press half of the mixture into a 9x5-inch meatloaf pan. Create a small trench down the middle of the meatloaf, and add cheese. Top with the remaining meatloaf mixture.

STEP 4
Combine the ketchup and balsamic vinegar in a small bowl, and brush on top of the meatloaf mixture. Bake for 55 minutes or until cooked through.

Big Daddy Devlin and MC

ANY SEASON

Florentine Turkey Meatloaf

PREP	COOK	SERVES
10 min	30 min	6

Rice Lombardy-Style

Shopping List

5½ cups chicken broth

2 tablespoons butter

½ teaspoon coarse sea salt

½ teaspoon freshly ground black pepper

2 cups Arborio rice

2 large egg yolks, room temperature

2 tablespoons olive oil

½ cup shredded Parmesan cheese

½ cup shredded Romano cheese

2 tablespoons fresh chopped sage

STEP 1 Heat broth, butter, salt and pepper to a boil over high heat in a heavy 4-quart saucepan. Stir in rice, and allow mixture to return to a boil, stirring occasionally.

STEP 2 Cover pot and reduce heat to low. Cook 15 minutes or until rice is al dente and mixture is a creamy texture like a risotto. If mixture is too thick, add more broth for desired texture.

STEP 3 Beat together egg yolks and oil in a small bowl, using a fork. Add Parmesan, and stir to form a paste. Set aside.

STEP 4 When rice is cooked, remove pot from heat. Stir in egg mixture, and stir vigorously until thoroughly blended. Stir in Romano and sage. Spoon rice into warm bowls, and garnish with fresh sage leaves.

notes:

Tip

To make 3-Cheese Rice Lombardy-Style, stir in ½ cup crumbled Gorgonzola cheese with Romano and sage in Step 3.

PREP	COOK	MAKES
20 min	20 min	32

Spinach and Feta Triangles

STEP 1 Preheat oven to 400°. Combine spinach, feta, cottage cheese, egg, dill, salt and pepper. Set aside.

STEP 2 Roll 1 sheet of pastry out on a floured surface to a 12-inch square, and cut it into 16 (3-inch) squares. Place a heaping tablespoon of spinach-feta mixture onto each square. Wet the edges with water, and fold the pastry over diagonally to form triangles, pressing well to seal. Crimp the edges with a fork. Repeat with remaining pastry and filling. Place on 2 parchment lined-baking sheets.

STEP 3 Bake for 20–22 minutes or until golden brown. Cool slightly, and serve.

Shopping List

1 (10-ounce) package frozen chopped spinach, thawed and squeezed dry

4 ounces feta cheese, crumbled

1 cup cottage cheese

1 egg

1 teaspoon dried dill or oregano

Salt and freshly ground pepper to taste

1 (17.3-ounce) package puff pastry sheets, thawed

MarkCharles Says:

"Start a new tradition and try new tastes by making this easy appetizer together with your whole family."

notes:

PREP
3 hrs 15 min

SERVES
10

No-Bake Raspberry Cheesecake

Shopping List

- 2 (8-ounce) packages cream cheese, softened
- 1 cup semisweet white chocolate chips, melted
- ⅓ cup sugar
- 2 cups whipped topping, thawed
- 2 cups frozen raspberries, thawed
- 1 (6-ounce) chocolate cookie pie crust

STEP 1 Beat cheese, chocolate and sugar in large bowl with a mixer until well blended. Whisk in whipped topping. Fold in raspberries. Spoon mixture into crust.

STEP 2 Refrigerate 3 hours.

Tip

Use 1 cup raspberry jam instead of frozen raspberries.

Marli, MC and Leo

notes:

PREP	SERVES
40 min	8

Turtle Brownie Cake

STEP 1 Prepare brownie mix according to package directions, and add half the jar of caramel sauce to the batter. Bake according to package directions in a greased 9x9-inch baking pan. Let cool.

STEP 2 Drizzle brownies with remaining caramel sauce and top with peanuts. Top with sprinkles. Cut into 3x1½-inch rectangles.

Shopping List

1 (16-ounce) box fudge brownie mix

1 (12-ounce) jar caramel sauce

¼ cup chopped peanuts

2 tablespoons chocolate sprinkles

Tip

Serve with vanilla or peanut butter ice cream.

PREP	FREEZE	SERVES
15 min	2 hrs	12

Easy Ice Cream Sandwich Cake

Shopping List

- 1 (12-count) box ice cream sandwiches
- 1 (11¾-ounce) jar hot fudge sauce
- 1 (½-gallon) tub rocky road ice cream (or any flavor), softened
- 2 cups whipped topping

STEP 1 Layer 13x9-inch pan with ice cream sandwiches. Spread ½ of the sauce on top. Freeze 30 minutes. Spread ice cream over sauce, then spread remaining sauce on top. Top with whipped topping.

STEP 2 Freeze 2 hours or overnight.

Tip

Top with strawberry ice cream sauce.

MarkCharles Says:

"Make this dessert the star for Family Night Dessert Share—everyone grab a long-handled iced tea spoon and "Deeg-in!"

notes:

PREP	SERVES
5 min	2

Kahlùa® Hazelnut Milkshake

STEP 1 Place ice cream, Kahlùa, and hazelnut spread in blender container.

STEP 2 Process 15–20 seconds or until completely smooth.

Shopping List

3 cups vanilla ice cream

1 tablespoon Kahlùa

1 tablespoon chocolate hazelnut spread

Tip

Recipe can be doubled.

notes:

Sonia, Preston and MC

PREP
30 min

SERVES
18

Easy Lemon Surprise Cupcakes

Shopping List

1 (18¼-ounce) package vanilla cake mix

2 cups whipped cream

1 (10-ounce) jar lemon curd

 STEP 1 Prepare cupcakes according to cake mix package directions, following cupcake method. Cool.

 STEP 2 Combine whipped cream and lemon curd in a medium mixing bowl. Place mixture in pastry bag.

 STEP 3 Insert tip of pastry bag down into cupcake and squeeze to fill center, then lift pastry bag out to release enough frosting for the top of cupcake.

Tip

Purchase store-bought unfrosted cupcakes instead of making cupcakes.

notes:

Coconut Rice Pudding with Pineapple
and Toasted Macadamia Nut Crumble

Any Season

PREP	COOK	SERVES
5 min	50 min	6

Coconut Rice Pudding with Pineapple and Toasted Macadamia Nut Crumble

STEP 1

For Pudding:
Combine rice, milk and sugar in a large saucepan. Bring to a boil. Lower heat, and simmer for 25–30 minutes or until rice is smooth and has a creamy texture.

STEP 2

Stir in coconut milk and shredded coconut. Simmer 10–12 minutes. Remove from heat, and cool in refrigerator for at least 1 hour.

STEP 3

Divide pudding into 6 bowls. Top each bowl with crumble topping and pineapple chunks.

STEP 4

For Topping:
Combine all ingredients in a small bowl. Spread on a baking sheet, and bake at 350° for 8–10 minutes or until lightly browned and crisp.

STEP 5

Remove from oven, and let cool completely. Crumble baked coconut mixture into small crumbs.

Shopping List

For Pudding:
1 cup Arborio rice

4 cups whole milk

½ cup sugar

1 (13½-ounce) can coconut milk

⅔ cup shredded sweetened coconut

For Topping:
¾ cup diced fresh pineapple chunks

½ cup chopped macadamia nuts

⅓ cup shredded and sweetened coconut

2 tablespoons melted butter

1½ tablespoons flour

1 tablespoon sugar

notes:

Mark and MC

ANY SEASON

"Deeg-In" • 195

Tropical Twist Wine Spritzer

Shopping List

1 cup white wine

¼ cup club soda

¼ cup guava juice (or your favorite tropical juice)

 STEP 1 Mix wine, club soda and juice in small pitcher. Pour into ice-filled glasses.

notes:

ANY SEASON

PREP
15 min

COOK
15 min

Cinnamon Hazelnut Mexican Wedding Bar Cookies

STEP 1 Cream butter, sugar and vanilla with a spoon; gradually blend in flour. Mix in nuts.

Press into bottom of 13x9-inch pan.

STEP 2
STEP 3 Bake in 325° oven for about 30 minutes or until cookies are creamy colored. Let cool until slightly warm, then remove from oven. Sprinkle with sugar.

Shopping List

1 cup butter or margarine, softened

¾ cup confectioners' sugar, with extra for sprinkling

1 teaspoon vanilla extract

2 cups all-purpose flour

½ teaspoon cinnamon

1 cup finely chopped hazelnuts

notes:

Tip

Substitute pecans or almonds for hazelnuts.

About the Author

MarkCharles Misilli has been in the kitchen products industry since 1993. With a background in product and interior design, he has worked in merchandising for several well-known major nationwide retailers as either a regional or national manager, in and with buying offices. Since 2001, he's also served as the "gadget expert" on QVC®.

As the host of *Kitchen Innovations with MarkCharles Misilli* on QVC, he shares his passion for making food prep fun and easy, and is in constant pursuit of bringing you "the better mouse-trap," as he frequently likes to say, whether through his own designs or finding unique products from his global travels.

MarkCharles has designed dozens of products under his brand MCM MarkCharles Misilli, for other major kitchenware brand names and for QVC, including gadgets, cookware and dinnerware. He is also partnering on some food items. This is his first cookbook under his brand name, and he has plans to create more.

In addition to his successes as a kitchen innovator and designer, MarkCharles has worked on hundreds of homes as an interior design specialist. He's served as a consultant on numerous projects for florists, law firms and advertising agencies. He also finds great joy in party planning, as he has been doing for the last twenty-five years with no formal training, combining his love of family and celebration.

Savory Sweet Potato Turnovers,
page 108

Index

Index

Index

Index

Index

notes: